Endorsements

Steve Darter's book reinforces for me the enormous value I extracted from the SIMA process and the understanding of my own MAP. The fundamental truths inherent in the principles of understanding and managing to one's MAP were waiting to be discovered and revealed. Steve's book elaborates on the value of applying these principles to the management of our own lives and to our effectiveness in managing others. I highly recommend the book to you."

Frederick J. Sievert
Vice Chairman
New York Life Insurance Company

"Regardless of where you are in your career - just starting out, somewhere in the middle, or nearing the end, this is a must read book. Your performance, the performance of your team, and the performance of the organization will dramatically improve if you apply the principles contained in this book. If you're not excited and energized after reading this book, check your pulse."

Richard G. Barnaby
Retired President and Chief Operating Officer
Kaiser Permanente

"As a result of the SIMA process, I have seen light bulbs go on as individuals realize what makes them tick. Steve is adept at capturing the essence of a person's strengths. It's uncanny how he is able to distill such pearls from the complexities that characterize people's life experiences. I have worked with Steve to profile leadership teams in two, top-tier companies. To a person, executives found the process extremely valuable and insightful. They continue to use MAP profiles to make staffing decisions, configure teams, and identify appropriate 'stretch assignments' for individuals."

Linda H. Lewis, Ed.D
Senior Vice President, Learning and Education
Charles Schwab & Company

Managing Yourself, Managing Others contains information, insights and understandings that will endure throughout one's business career, and beyond. A truly impactful approach to understanding business and personal motivations and success factors."

James E. Miller
Executive Vice President
MassMutual Financial Group

"To learn what motivates you and your people to be effective and advance your organization, invest the time to read Steve Darter's book. Steve can bring sound methods to help you optimize your people power."

R.Channing Wheeler
Chief Executive Officer, Uniprise
A UnitedHealth Group Company

Endorsements

"SIMA and People Management have been enormously helpful to me and the organizations I have served. I recommend the firm and their techniques often when change is needed. People's gifts and God given talents are described accurately by SIMA. It is a practical approach that honors the individual. I had my SIMA done over twenty five years ago and I still appreciate the insights."

Albert Quie
Former Governor, Minnesota

"Not just very interesting and intriguing reading, but a very useful and practical tool. We used SIMA extensively for managerial hiring, internal moves and promotions as well as career planning. We found it to be very accurate, and it should definitely be considered as a great predictive tool for job fit and successful assignments. I used to tell my staff 'make sure this person gets 'Darterized' before we make a final decision."

Herman Fonteyne
Retired President & CEO
Ensign-Bickford Industries, Inc.

"This book addresses the very core of managing and presents the finest tool I've seen that promotes human development within the work place."

Joseph Carlone
President and General Manager
Linemaster Switch Corporation

"This concise and richly illustrated book is a must read for anyone interested in improving performance and enhancing motivation at work. Whether the focus of your interest is on yourself, your direct reports, or coaching others how to realize rewards from their work efforts you will find sage advice throughout this book from one of the premier career consultants working today."

James W. Fairfield-Sonn, Ph.D.
President
Fairfield-Sonn Associates

"Managing Yourself, Managing Others is a must read for anyone who cares to fully comprehend and then optimize their own innate motivational forces or those of their employees. Darter has given us a wonderfully written treatise on a subject that has the unusual dimension of pertaining to everyone."

Dr. William B Sherwood
Vice President HR, Administration, & Infrastructure
Philips Research Labs

"A very powerful tool to improved productivity and enjoying your work. It has application to yourself, your employees, and your family – put it to good use!!!"

Eric B. Warming
Global Engineering Director
Dupont Dow Elastomers

"When I was first introduced to SIMA, I thought it was just going to be another packaged approach to self discovery. However, it is, by far, the most productive assessment and personal awareness tool I have ever used. Even now, more than two years later, I pull my copy of my MAP out from time to time to make sure that I'm still focusing on my motivated abilities. This book distills the entire process and its value thoroughly but clearly, and is a must read."

Thomas Kilby
Former President
Waring Products

"The book is excellent, enjoyable to read, and full of worthwhile information."

Richard Sugarman
Founding President
The Connecticut Forum

"It was my pleasure and privilege to read your manuscript. Your approach to leadership affirms the individual's energy, culture, wisdom, and encourages self-direction. I found your work to be both challenging and courageous. For persons facing decisions, career changes, or seeking meaning in their lives, your work is a solid foundation that uses the crucial threads of their life to develop and achieve the framework for their beliefs and choices. Your work is insightful, unusual, intelligent, and interesting.

Marylouise Fennell, RSM, Ed.D
Senior Consultant, Council of Independent Colleges
Past President, Carlow College (PA)

"Steve explains a structured process to apply common sense principles to the most important decisions we make regarding our careers. Motivation is the compelling variable that underlies our ultimate successes, failures, contentment and frustrations. This book teaches us how to understand and use our personal motivations to manage our careers and the careers of the people we manage. The insights are immediately applicable, thanks."

Jerry Gotthainer
President
Ascendia Health

"Steve Darter's book, *Managing Yourself, Managing Others,* brilliantly captures the relevance and value of linking individual potential to the needs of organizations. He successfully uses the SIMA technology as the catalyst for identifying motivated abilities and optimizing the organization's human resources by focusing them on achieving business objectives. Truly a win-win strategy."

Alfred G. Wilke
Retired Vice President, Human Resources
Travelers Property Casualty Company

"I have found SIMA to clarify the basic strengths that people bring to their work. I have used SIMA in my own personal decision making, with members of my family, in staffing my offices and I often recommend People Management to clients in my current consulting practice."

David Durenberger
Former US Senator, Minnesota

"In today's highly competitive, rapidly changing, global marketplace, the effective use of people has never been more critical. In *Managing Yourself, Managing Others,* Steve Darter provides a concise way to understand each individual's strengths and Motivated Abilities Pattern (MAP). The flatter organizations in favor today require that each employee has increased responsibility for bottom line performance. Similarly, the increased use of teams to shorten cycle times requires that employees work together effectively. The manager must understand each employee's strengths and weaknesses and what motivates their efforts in order to place people in the right position in the organization and to form effective teams. Steve provides a direct way to assess the motivational patterns of employees. The proper application of this process can result in more effective, satisfied employees and a more competitive organization. Steve's common sense presentation makes it easy to understand and apply the System for Identifying Motivated Abilities (SIMA) with your employees and yourself."

George Burman, Ph.D.
Dean, School of Management
Syracuse University

"Seventeen years ago I completed the Motivated Abilities program (SIMA) with Steve Darter. It provided me with some very interesting 'sign posts' to watch for in my corporate activities and since then, I've been struck by the accuracy of the programs conclusions related to the matching of my personal characteristics. Most importantly, in those cases where potential mismatches might have otherwise created major problems or concerns for me, I've found that I've been prepared and able to manage them effectively."

David C Tiemeier, Ph.D.
Vice President, Pharmaceutical Leasing
Searle, A Monsanto Company

"In the years since I went through the SIMA process, I've found it extremely valuable in dealing with people whom I have come in contact with through my consulting experience. It has also proved to underscore for me what types of working environments are best suited for me and what types of situations were uncomfortable and caused me to struggle. My only real regret is that I was so far along in my working life that some of my lesser rewarding assignments could have been avoided had I known of the potential of the SIMA system earlier in my career."

William G. Holbrook
Former Executive Director
Association for Manufacturing Excellence

"I have been an advocate for SIMA and People Management for the last nine years, as CEO of two health care organizations. SIMA provides a view of how individuals will actually do the work. Its accuracy and predictive descriptions is almost uncanny. My most recent organizations have used SIMA to assess over 500 individuals for critical leadership assessment, selection and succession planning."

Richard Norling
Chief Executive Officer
Premier

"The basic idea of finding out what people are driven to do well and then developing their jobs around those abilities is a uniquely simple, but elegant concept. The elegance resides in the fact that many people don't know what they are motivated to do well, nor do their supervisors. This is the fact that gives the System For Identifying Motivated Abilities a unique value, because it allows the unlocking of a new depth of human resources that would otherwise go undiscovered and untapped. I have used this basic approach for the past 15 years and found it to be tremendously rewarding—to the individual and our company."

Stephen D. Ban, Ph.D.
President and CEO
Gas Research Institute

"I have seen the results of SIMA and People Management's consulting in two organizations where I serve as a board member. In search and selection planning applications for hard leadership choices, SIMA has given critical insights."

James Bere
President
Alta Resources

Managing Yourself, Managing Others clearly delivers on its promise of providing a new way to understand and manage people. It is a critical read and 'must have' resource for those leaders who seriously want to be more successful managing others and themselves."

John Madigan
Information Technology – Human Resources
Hartford Financial Services Group

"If you have ever questioned how some employees seem to fit so magically with their job, while other people are always at odds with theirs, *Managing Yourself, Managing Others* is a must read. As an educator, manager and former management school dean, I have encountered hundreds of people at all ages, who have spent too much time stuck in either a personal career crossroad or in poor fit management or staff positions. Steven Darter has captured the essence of 'best fit' and this book would have been a powerful resource to them."

Alyce Gould
Director of Education and Development
New Britain General Hospital
Former Associate Dean, School of Management
Hartford Graduate Center

"As I made my personal decision to leave my business career and join World Vision, I found the results of my SIMA assessment very helpful in reinforcing my call to this ministry. We have used SIMA and People Management extensively to assure job fit and performance at the senior levels."

Richard Stearns
President
World Vision United States

"We have used People Management and the SIMA process through several stages of our company's development and growth. At each critical juncture, SIMA has provided helpful insight as our business has changed."

Ruth Hiaring Wreisner
Vice President of Compliance and Human Resources
Bankers Systems

"In 1985 I found myself at crossroads whether to continue in management or return to the technical career ladder. Keeping perceptions, feelings, and opinions out of the decision making appeared impossible until I had the opportunity to go through the SIMA process. I am most grateful for this since it helped me to make an important career decision that has proven right for me."

Bjorn Tyreus
Research Fellow
DuPont Corporate R&D

"The SIMA process is the most detailed and in-depth assessment I have discovered. It gives understanding to both individuals and their organizations for good planning and decision making. At CCCU several colleges are exploring how to use the process with students to help in retention."

Robert Andringa
President
Council of Christian Colleges and Universities

"In making my move to Fairview, SIMA and the advice of People Management were critical to the decision. Our senior team has used SIMA to understand the strengths of senior team members prior to selection."

David Page
Chief Executive Officer
Fairview Health System

"Fortunately Steve Darter introduced me to SIMA as I was retiring from a long career in healthcare management. I used the understanding of my Motivational Pattern to create a consulting firm, and the result has been very satisfying and financially successful."

Sam Havens
Retired President, Prudential Healthcare
Former Chairman of the American Association of Health Plans

"I was introduced to SIMA over ten years ago as a way to help young professionals find their optimum career path. I participated personally to fully understand its benefits and found it to be extremely enlightening in what I am motivated to do and how I like to get work done. I continue to use the results today both in my professional life and my personal life to improve my effectiveness and to make career decisions. I would recommend SIMA to anyone who wants to go deeper than just surveys and questionnaires to understand their motivations."

Bradford F. Dunn
Senior Purchasing Agent
E.I. du Pont de Nemours and Company

"The SIMA process described in Steve's book provided me direction and focus during my job search. It assisted me in identifying the correct position and company."

William Wolf
President
Delta Systems Designs, Inc.

Managing Yourself, Managing Others

STEVEN M. DARTER

MANAGING YOURSELF, MANAGING OTHERS

© 2001, Steven M. Darter

First Edition
Strong Books
615 Queen Street
Southington, CT 06489

ISBN: 1-928782-25-6
Library of Congress Catalog Card Number: 00-110725

Cover Design: Ellen Gregory
Book Design: Kathryn-Ann O'Brien

A Tribute

This book is a tribute to Arthur F. Miller Jr. and his life-long devotion to spreading the word about giftedness and the part it plays in the lives of us all.

I met Art in 1975 at a conference where he was a presenter introducing SIMA® (the System for Identifying Motivated Abilities). What Art said about people hit a core within my professional and personal spirit. This chance meeting and Art's wisdom and counsel helped me to see a path to walk down—which I did—and to him, I will be forever grateful.

Prologue

Art Miller Jr. asked me to endorse this book. And I do. But what I am really endorsing (and what Steve Darter is telling you about in this book) is arguably the best instrument available to you to understand the dynamics of people and jobs: The process known as SIMA® (System for Identifying Motivated Abilities).

There are three threads to my personal experience with SIMA:

- What SIMA has meant to me;
- How I have used SIMA; and
- How I should have used SIMA.

What SIMA has meant to me. My first encounter with SIMA was on a long plane trip, with the SIMA Biographical Form as my designated time killer. I was flying back to corporate headquarters, basking in my recent appointment to an executive position in my company. I fully expected SIMA to be yet another dose of corporate sheep-dip—simply a check mark on my executive development checklist.

My first surprise came with the SIMA form itself. Imagine recounting experiences from way back in your childhood—or even ten years ago—or other times mostly ignored by corporate programs. I was mystified. What possible value would these experiences have in my march to corporate stardom?

My next surprises came in the next few weeks as the interviews and discussions with Art Miller Jr. unfolded. I learned I was motivated by things foreign to my corporate climb. I was tactical, not strategic. I was conceptual, not detailed. I was fluid, not structured. And I was a change agent, not a goal achiever.

This all struck a very discordant tune with me. After all, aren't corporate biggies supposed to be strategic? Detailed? Structured? Achievement-oriented? If so, what am I doing here? The answer came to me indirectly, through the biggest influence in my professional life, my mentor, a gifted executive by the name of Ernie Ridenhour.

It turned out that Ernie possessed all the motivated abilities I did not—strategic thinking; attention to details; a structured approach; and oriented to goals. And he had used these motivations to achieve great success over his forty-year career in our company. He also used them to deal with me. Over time, with a lot of coaching, I came to realize my role was to be the Patton to my mentor's Eisenhower in our corporate "warfare."

And so we went to war—my mentor armed with the vision and political skills, me armed with the motivation to operate effectively under his corporate air cover. And SIMA was our secret weapon. (More on this later.)

It is now some 10 years after this epoch in my life. My mentor is retired and an e-mail away. I have moved on to consulting, leaving the battlefield to the younger generations. (In the ultimate of ironies, I have recognized—after the fact and after 30 years of doing otherwise—that consulting is the field best suited to my motivated abilities.)

To this day, I keep a strong mental model of my motivated abilities with me at all times. Not surprisingly, I am still Patton, doing war for an Eisenhower. (In consulting, my Eisenhower is the aura of expertise and experience carried by my company's well-deserved reputation.) Do I use SIMA all the time? No. But do I recognize its enduring message to me? You bet. I have used the power of SIMA to aid my growth, and the balm of SIMA to help understand (not excuse) my missteps and failures.

How I have used SIMA. In addition to the application of SIMA in my professional life, I have helped use SIMA in two broader organizational contexts: restructuring a business unit and measuring the fit of an existing management team.

Restructuring:

Our corporation was embracing Total Quality Management in a big way, and my business unit—a large internal information services bureau—was operating "against the grain." We were too internally focused, too expensive, and too unresponsive to our customers. Under the guidance and vision of my mentor; we embarked on a massive restructuring of the bureau. All management positions in the bureau were redefined and put up for grabs.

We began a massive internal candidate hunt that allowed people throughout the corporation to apply for one of the new positions. Once we narrowed down the candidate list, we employed the SIMA process on the remaining candidates to help us match the attributes of the positions with the motivated abilities of the candidates. Post-SIMA candidate interviews and serious executive discussion facilitated by Art Miller Jr. and his PMI team completed the selection process.

Team Fit:

In another corporation, our group's management team was suffering. Conflict was rampant. Progress was stifled. Teamwork seemed non-existent. The rest of the company was not comfortable with our services or us.

As part of our solution, we turned to SIMA. Each member of the management team received a Motivated Abilities Pattern (MAP) and some careful coaching about understanding and appreciating differences. Also, the executive team (me included) received some good guidance about which assignments were the best fits to the incumbents' MAPS.

As a result of these sessions, we gently restructured the management team—reassigning some members to positions of better fit and realigning reporting relationships to take advantage of complementary (or reinforcing) MAPs.

The end results were predictable but welcome nonetheless: smoother internal relationships; less friction; more cooperation. And ultimately, we had the opportunity to position our group in a more strategic role within the company.

How I should have used SIMA. I feel strongly that ignoring the messages of SIMA is an invitation to misfortune. Nonetheless, I have ignored them in certain situations.

In my professional life, I have taken assignments that I knew to be mismatches, figuring I could turn them into fulfilling roles. Many of us have done this. But I should know better. Not only am I pushing against one of the basic tenets of SIMA, but also I am not recognizing one of my MAP traits—the blind faith in my own ability to make things the way I want them!

But perhaps the way I should have used my SIMA knowledge is to understand others better. Understanding oneself is not enough. What motivates me does not necessarily motivate others. And nowhere did this become more evident than in my personal life.

I had the great fortune to "find" a family well into my life. I married a beautiful person and became a father to her three lovely children in my 40s. Our life has been generally wonderful. But I regret the opportunities I have missed to listen to my wife and children, not with the filter of my own motivations, but instead with an appreciation of theirs. Far worse, I have wasted untold amounts of energy attempting to foist my motivations on them rather than helping them understand their own. Fortunately they have survived (and thrived) in spite of my failings.

Conclusion. All in all, I have found my journey with SIMA to be a life-defining experience. In my opinion, it's the best tool to understand the dynamics of individuals in corporations. It's also the best tool to understand yourself. The good people of PMI (Art Miller Jr. and Steven Darter, in particular) have generously shared the process and insights with you through this book. Take advantage of their generosity.

–Drew Blanchard
Former General Manager of
McDonnell Douglas Aerospace Information Services and
currently a principal consultant with Computer Sciences Corporation

Did You Know That?

- *Fewer than 1 out of every 4 jobholders say that they are currently working at full potential.*

- *One-half said they do not put effort into their job over and above what is required to hold onto it.*

- *The overwhelmingly majority, 75 percent, said that they could be significantly more effective than they presently are.*

– Warren Bennis & Burt Nanus
Leaders: The Strategies for Taking Charge

Contents

Preface

This book started to take shape twenty-five years ago when the first person I worked with as a consultant said to me, "I really don't know what went wrong—why they fired me." Since then I have interviewed, met, and consulted with thousands of executives and managers and, through their eyes, have seen the paths that people have taken that led to success or to dissatisfaction and failure. On the following pages I am going to share with you some of what I have learned about achieving success personally and helping others and one's organization to be successful.

What I learned from that executive is that he was fired because he didn't manage himself well, and as a result, didn't manage others well, and as a result, didn't manage his part of the organization well. And he didn't come to realize it until it seemed to him like his life was crumbling.

In brief, this book is about how to be a more effective manager of people and yourself and how to create an environment that brings forth the "best" that people have to give. If you can learn to effectively manage yourself and others, then you will have a greater chance to achieve success and to help others and your organization to be successful.

Introduction

For some people, this book will be about helping their organizations to improve performance by tapping into the heart and soul of their employees. For others, it will be about finding a place in this world where they can feel productive and alive—where what they do has meaning, satisfaction, and a sense of purpose and fulfillment. For all, this book will be about understanding and using a force (a motivational force) that resides inside all of us, that can lift us to enormous heights or sink us to despair if not managed properly.

By listening to this force and using it as a guide, you will become a more effective manager of yourself. By understanding this force and its dynamics within others, you will become a more effective manager of people.

Each of us has giftedness, purpose, and an innate motivational drive, and when we uncover it (or stumble upon it or into it) our life, for that moment, has a sense of congruence and fit. The more we can operate in that zone, which brings forth the energy and fire within, the more meaningful our life feels.

The practicality of this to organizations is that when employees are in roles that tap into their giftedness and purpose, they are more satisfied and productive. The more an organization is seeded (at all levels) with people who do their jobs with passion, the more effective it will be. This book will help as you strive to create such an organization.

In the course of helping you to understand how to tap into the passion of your employees and, by doing so, how it impacts organizations, I am also going to describe how you can discover the passion and energy within you. If you make this investment, you will be a more effective manager of others and yourself. If you make this investment, you may also find, as a result, that your life will take on more meaning and your path to success will be easier to find.

The way I am going to achieve this is by telling you about a way to understand people and how to use that understanding to be a more effective manager. In Chapters One and Two, I begin by introducing a process called SIMA® (System for Identifying Motivated Abilities). Through SIMA, you can identify a MAP® (Motivated Abilities Pattern) which is a description of how a person is most highly motivated. I begin this introduction to SIMA and its value to individuals and organizations by describing my initial encounter with Arthur F. Miller Jr., who is the founder of SIMA.

Chapter Three will give you a better understanding of how a MAP is constructed so that you can better understand how to identify and use the Motivational Pattern that is within you and the Motivational Patterns that reside within your employees.

In Chapter Four, the meaning and implications of Motivational Patterns are explained which show how they profoundly affect the lives of people and organizations. Chapter Five is devoted to showing how knowledge of Motivational Patterns can be used to improve: performance, job fit, work satisfaction, the learning process, and relationships. Chapter Six is devoted to helping you understand SIMA and Motivational Patterns within a larger context.

The process of constructing one's MAP is briefly described in Appendix A. Appendix B introduces the People Management organization and its network of twenty-eight worldwide consulting organizations. People Management companies use SIMA to assist organizations and individuals on issues related to job fit and the effective use of talent. Appendix C is a Bibliography of SIMA for those who wish to read more, and Appendix D summarizes most of the research that has been conducted on the SIMA process.

If you are experiencing difficulty in your organization or with people or with performance (yours or others) or not feeling particularly motivated or just want to understand how to be a more effective manager of yourself and others, then this book will provide a lot of useful information.

If you live your life with the belief that people are expendable and not worth the effort, then this book is not for you, unless, you wish to be challenged on those beliefs.

Effective management is the productive use of strengths.

–Peter Drucker

Chapter I

The Path Emerges
and the Foundation Laid

Have you ever considered this incredible fact inherent in our two foundational institutions of education and work? A person is educated for fifteen or so years . . . hired in a job . . . and then for half a century is rewarded, punished, utilized, directed, coached, managed, trained, appraised, developed, reinforced, promoted, transferred, harnessed to objectives, subjected to job enrichment and enlargement activities . . . sent to business school, assessment centers, sensitivity training . . . promoted, etc. . . . . and finally retired – WITHOUT ANYBODY – AT ANY TIME – FINDING OUT WHAT THAT PERSON IS REALLY GOOD AT AND MOTIVATED TO DO.

Arthur F. Miller Jr.

He was telling me about all of his success—the title, the office, the power, the financial results, and personal financial payoff—up from the bottom to the top. A modern day Horatio Algier story. He was beaming, and I was happy for him.

We didn't stay in touch much. I was a consultant, and other organizations and assignments kept me busy. When I traveled to his city, I tried to visit, but our schedules didn't mesh. I kept him on my mailing list, and periodically sent information about my company or an article I thought he might find of interest. It was about four years after that day when he called asking to meet.

After exchanging a few minutes of pleasantries, he got right to the problem. "It's going okay," he said, "but I sense that the organization is slipping away. . . . I've lost a few key people, results aren't quite as good, morale doesn't seem right. . . . I'm not in any jeopardy, but I don't think i'm as effective as I could be."

I asked him to describe the organization and the people and the issues that he saw. Then I asked him to describe himself and how he interacted with his people and the organization. I asked how he thought others would describe him and how he led, managed, and interacted with the organization.

I questioned the picture that he was painting and helped him to explore and probe the myriad of thoughts in his mind. What value did he bring—when, where, how?

In preparation of the meeting, I reviewed the assessment we had done years earlier when the company was deciding whether to hire him or not. I referred back to the assessment to help him to better understand himself. I showed him how he could improve his performance by restructuring how he spent his time and where he put his energy and focus. It was a productive three hours.

He admitted that he had not looked at, nor could he find, the assessment. He asked for a fresh copy. He suggested ways my company might be of help inside his company. He was intrigued about the way we look at people and try to understand what motivates them to perform their best. We went to lunch, and he asked about how I got involved with People Management and SIMA. I began by telling him about Arthur F. Miller Jr. and his ideas and beliefs.

This is where I am going to begin as I describe my thoughts about how to be a more effective manager of people and yourself.

What is Motivational Patterning?

I first met Arthur F. Miller Jr. in 1975 while attending a conference at Bucknell University. He was a guest speaker and I was an attendee. He arrived late and was stumbling around looking for his conference host. I responded to his locational bewilderment and disorientation by asking if I could be of assistance. We began to talk.

If you have ever met Art, you would know firsthand what happened next. I innocently asked him what he was speaking about the next day— and for the next several hours we were engaged in a conversation about people, motivation, giftedness, and human design, the likes of which I had never heard before. He was argumentative, stubborn, intriguing, highly passionate, and very compelling.

I decided to attend his presentation the next day. I watched him debate, argue, and defend his beliefs before a packed room. What he said astounded me, and I was drawn to learn more.

Art was kind enough to open his files to my curiosity, and I dug into cases that were richly documented. I tried my hand at using his techniques and following his principles. The thing that repeatedly struck me was how accurate and simple his discoveries were. Yet, within the simplicity there was depth and complexity. Art was on to something, and I was being drawn into it.

Art has spent much of his adult life interviewing people and helping them and organizations to make wiser decisions, initially, as director of personnel at Argonne National Labs and later at Raytheon and

Combustion Engineering. In 1961 he formed People Management which provided executive search and recruiting management services to corporations.

Although Art started a firm that helped organizations to acquire technical professionals, his focus and intention was to explore a belief that he had about people and work.

Through his interviews, he saw that each person seemed to have his or her own natural style and that when a person didn't work out in a job, it generally had much more to do with style and issues of compatibility than it did with a lack of technical background or experience. He began to see that each person was different, unique, an individual, a snowflake, a thumbprint, and that much of one's satisfaction and success at work was tied into using what appeared to be one's natural gifts and abilities.

Art pursued this observation and discovered that residing within each of us is a natural pattern of motivation which triggers us to perform our best, which sustains us and drives us, but for each person the pattern is different. He called this phenomena a Motivated Abilities Pattern® (MAP).

What Is the Importance of Understanding Motivational Patterns?

Art found that each person's Motivational Pattern emerged early in that person's life and stayed constant—that people tend to perceive the world through their unique Patterns and attempt to perform jobs in a way that allows them to exercise their Patterns—that when people work in jobs that play into their MAPs, they tend to excel, and when they are put into work that is opposite their MAPs, they tend to become frustrated and perform poorly. He saw that each person had a core within them that was foundational to who they were.

He came to believe that people were not putty to be molded and shaped. They were not blank sheets of paper to be written upon. He recognized the profound impact that life experiences had on individuals, but he also saw that despite the comfort or extremity of one's environment, the essence of a person's MAP remained constant. He began to use the word "design" because what he saw within each person was deeper and more meaningful than just skills or abilities. He saw a pattern of behavior that continually repeated itself—that tried to repeat itself despite the environment or living conditions that it found itself within, and this had significant implications for people and the organizations in which they worked.

As he climbed into organizations, he saw that poor performance, more often than not, was the result of people either being in jobs that did not fit them well or using their MAPs in such a way that negative consequences resulted.

As he listened to people review their lives, he realized that the essence of success and satisfaction for each person came as they embraced their MAP, developed it, and made use of it. When people spoke of their greatest successes, they described their MAPs that were unique to them. And when they spoke of failure and frustration, he saw that their MAPs were often denied expression and were not allowed to flourish.

He saw that as organizations tapped into the motivated strengths of their employees, that they would be more successful.

The truth in what Art realized is all around us. As managers, we can look at our employees and see their differences. We can see how one person focuses on detail, while another is more conceptual. We see how some are team-oriented and others loners—how some are talkers, and others writers. There are those who are good with numbers, those good with organizing things, and on and on—and as managers, we take those differences and strengths into consideration and use them to improve productivity and performance (hopefully).

As individual workers, we can look at ourselves and see that there are aspects to our work that we enjoy doing and can't wait to get to, and sometimes we do this work first, even though it's not a priority, simply because we enjoy doing it. Likewise, there are other aspects of our work that we can do but, in some ways, we need to put some rawhide between our teeth in order to do it, or at least to discipline ourselves. Sometimes this work ends up on the bottom of the pile until it is absolutely necessary that it be done.

If you look, you can see natural talent and giftedness all around. An obvious example is the natural athlete, like Michael Jordan, or the natural teacher or the natural salesperson. But what about the rest of us? Are we void of natural talent, somehow left out? What about the natural listener, or the natural organizer, or the person who's just naturally good at putting someone at ease?

It's easy to see the talent of Michael Jordan and be thrilled watching him create moves on a basketball court. But giftedness in any place can be exhilarating. Think of going into a restaurant and the difference between having a wait person who is merely there versus one who is naturally gifted in serving and taking care of others, and how we notice that and comment upon it, and how much better the meal tastes because of it. And how the good or poor job fit of that one wait person can impact the success of the organization.

Natural talent and giftedness in the right place takes root. For example, the leader who steps in to establish vision, direction, and a sense of purpose when the organization is floundering; the organizer who structures work when chaos prevails; the influencer who carries the message, spreads the word, and gets others on board. Natural talent and giftedness is truly a wonder to behold when used in the right place. However, when it is in the wrong place, it is awkward—not quite right. It becomes a weakness and, in many ways, a weakness is nothing more than the flip side of someone's natural strengths.

For example, think of the analytical person, someone who wants to weigh things carefully, to really think about things in depth, who wants to be really sure, who wants to make well-thought-out, "right" decisions. Imagine that person in a start-up where he or she can't get access to all the information, where he or she needs to make quick decisions, needs to go with gut and feel. What was a strength becomes a potential weakness.

Think about the relationship builder, the person who prides him or herself on building relationships, who cherishes the relationships, and works hard at developing and maintaining them. Imagine that person being in charge of a turnaround situation where he or she needs to make tough decisions regarding people. What was a strength becomes a potential weakness.

Think of the person who likes to change things, likes to drive change, to imagine change, who sees how things need to be changed. Imagine putting that person in charge of running a very smooth-functioning operation.

Art believes that each person should be aware of his or her MAP and that each person should continually refer to it when making decisions about his or her life. He also believes that each organization should understand the MAPs of its employees and use the information to make decisions. If people and organizations did that, then, as he has so passionately articulated for almost forty years, there would be a lot more success.

How Do You Identify Motivational Patterns?

The process that Art developed to identify one's MAP is called SIMA® (the System for Identifying Motivated Abilities). Briefly, this is how it works.

You start by asking the person to generate a list of achievements—situations that individual has been in where he or she has done something that was enjoyed and felt was done well. You ask the person to write down achievements that cover his or her lifetime—some from childhood through the teenage years and into adulthood. If the person is young, then these achievements are all concentrated in a brief time period.

You then interview the person on those achievements. In that interview, you are attempting to find out what was happening that was giving this person such a tremendous sense of satisfaction and success.

The interview is very different in that it is not a probing one. You don't ask, "Did you do this?" or "Did you do that?" The interview process is actually quite passive. You purposely avoid your own curiosity. You try to stay out of the person's way and let them tell their story in their own words.

What you're saying to the person being interviewed is, "Tell me what you did and how you went about doing it," and then you listen. As the person describes how he or she went about doing things, phrases emerge like: "I built, I designed, I managed, I planned, I communicated"; and as the individual uses those words, you stop and ask: "How? How did you build it, how did you design it, how did you manage it, how did you plan it, climb up the mountain, beat up the bully, hit the home run, save the day, make the sale, get the project done?—describe how." And as the person does, what happens is that you can see a theme emerge early in his or her life and remain very, very constant throughout that individual's life.

Seeing each person's MAP unfold and recognizing its inherence and centrality to his or her life is an astounding experience.

How Can You Use What You Will Learn About Motivational Patterning?

First let me say that since 1961, collectively within the People Management organization, we have interviewed over 75,000 people and have never seen two MAPs exactly the same. From a very practical perspective, what we say to people when we help them to make decisions about their own work lives is, "If this is the kind of stuff, the kinds of things, the kinds of themes, that have given you this tremendous sense of satisfaction and success in the past, then you ought to look for work that allows you to use as much of your MAP as you possibly can."

As consultants to organizations, what we say to our clients is, "You are much better off putting people into positions for which they are naturally motivated—that way, the organization benefits as well as the people themselves."

We also say to our clients, "When someone is performing poorly or the team is in disharmony or there is conflict between two people or stuff is not being done properly, then you can look at the situation through the eyes of SIMA." What is revealed often sheds new light and new insight that, if used properly, can be of enormous value.

In terms of immediate value—once you recognize that people already have patterns of what motivates them, then you can begin to look at people and issues related to performance with a different perspective and, with that insight, become a more effective manager.

For example, as a boss, you can deal more effectively with your subordinates; as a worker, more effectively with your peers; as a leader, more effectively with your troops; as an employee, more effectively with your boss.

The value of SIMA can even help you to better understand and manage relationships outside of work: as a parent, you can better understand and deal more effectively with your children; as a spouse, more effectively with your mate; as a child, more effectively with your parents, and on and on.

As you better understand the principles, techniques, and implications of SIMA and MAPs, you will be better able to look at people and ask, "What is really at the heart of this person? What is truly motivating him or her, or motivating to yourself?" And with that knowledge and understanding, comes better decision making regarding relationships, the use of people, and the use of yourself.

Let me now return to that executive that I briefly told you about at the start of this chapter. As we shook hands and said our good-byes, he thanked me for the suggestions. He then said that he had not realized until that day how important it was to try and understand the people in his organization and what motivates them (rather than assume that they could, or would, merely adapt to roles and assignments). He also realized how important it was to understand what motivates him to be most successful and the value of continuing the process of learning how to manage his strengths so that they don't become weaknesses. He observed, correctly I might add, that doing so is a life-long, developmental process.

He was already successful when I met him, but as a result of his understanding his MAP and better managing it, he experienced even more success. Rather than stumbling or falling off the path, he had a better sense in which direction to head.

CHAPTER II

The Path To Success
Starts With a MAP

Alice: *"Which way ought I walk from here?"*

Cat: *"That depends a good deal on where you want to get to."*

Alice: *"I don't much care where."*

Cat: *"Then it doesn't matter which way you walk."*

–From Alice in Wonderland

I had just finished providing the president with the results of my assessment of the two finalists for a position as senior vice president of marketing. It was clear to me that one of the candidates was a better choice given the selection criteria that had been laid out for me by the vice president of human resources. This was my first meeting with the CEO because the assessment needed to be done quickly and time limitations did not permit us the opportunity to meet beforehand. Given the fact that he didn't know much about me and my approach, I was trying not to be absolute in my beliefs. My approach was mainly to ask questions and to point things out, to help him see what was clear to me.

I tried to help him understand the importance of job fit and tapping into the Motivational Pattern of a person—how, if an individual is not in work that fits with the essence of who he or she is, then you only get a piece of what the person has to give. I explained that the more the person and work were aligned, the more passionate and productive the person would be.

He leaned back in his chair and gently placed his head onto his fingers. His eyes drifted as he pursued thoughts in his mind. He then moved forward, looked me square in the eyes with the strength of a tough negotiator and said, "I need to do something different with my life. I'm thinking of buying an inn in Vermont and running it. Do you think it's a good idea?"

I asked him why he was contemplating doing this. He spoke of how he used to like the work that he did but that it was becoming less meaningful for him, and as it did, he felt that he was being less effective in that he had to discipline himself to work harder and harder in order to do the work well. At the end of each day, he said he was so totally drained that he didn't have any energy left to do anything else. The idea of running an inn seemed so appealing.

One of the most important responsibilities you have as a manager of your own life is to try to put yourself into work situations that enable you to feel good about yourself and the work you are doing. One of the most important responsibilities you have as a manager of others is to help people to find roles that enable them to be most productive to the organizations which employ them.

What the president said to me was not unusual and, in many ways, was quite typical.

I have found in my consulting that people often begin journeys by looking to get away from something. They know that the situations that they are in are uncomfortable, and they want to relieve that discomfort. In their attempts to get out of bad situations and into something new, their ability to evaluate options is skewed. Situations that might not otherwise look attractive seem to hold far more promise than they should. The excitement of the new or different or unknown, or the imagination of what could be, takes over. What might not make the cut now occupies center stage.

The preceding dialogue from *Alice in Wonderland* drives home the point that you and your employees need some sort of beacon as a guide— some sort of image or criteria to use when evaluating how to invest one's energy and the direction of one's life.

If this criteria emerges from someone else's image of what you or your employees should be or do, then it will most likely end in disappointment. There are many blind alleys and roads to nowhere. People need to assume responsibility for their own lives and good managers ought to help them. People need to draw their own MAPs. They need to be their own navigators and to be their own pilots. This doesn't mean that they travel alone or don't seek the guidance of others. That would be naive.

My point is, if people don't have an understanding of what is important to them, of what gives them that feeling of success, then finding one's path to success will be more difficult.

If, after reading this book you are interested in identifying aspects of your own Motivational Pattern, you can begin your journey by listing your achievements—those situations in your life where you did something that you enjoyed doing and felt that you did well.

Beginning on page 132 is the form we, at People Management, use to assist individuals in this first step. Once you complete this form, you will then be asked to follow a process that involves Achievement Interviewing[SM]. This is a very disciplined interviewing process where the details of how you went about accomplishing your achievements are brought forth.

The data from the achievement interview is then used to identify the recurring motivational themes in your life. These are the themes that come together to form your MAP.

In Appendix A, various techniques for drawing your MAP are presented as well as specific rules regarding MAP construction and Achievement Interviewing.

By the way, the president didn't buy an inn in Vermont, and he didn't quit the company or leave his job. What he did was restructure his job so that he could concentrate on doing what he was motivated to do best.

CHAPTER III

MAP Composition

Geniuses are the luckiest of mortals because what they must do is the same as what they most want to do.

–W. H. Auden

One of the differences between SIMA and almost every test that looks to describe people is that there are no predetermined categories or types with SIMA. It is an open system.

At People Management, we believe that everyone is motivated by different things. Yes, we could cluster people into types, but once that is done, then a person is being fit into a predefined box.

We tailor descriptions to fit a person. We do this by listening to the individual's achievements, and through his or her words, describing the phenomena that appear.

This does not suggest that tests are not accurate or don't have a place, but when the test focuses on a generalized description, then we feel that the uniqueness of the individual is lost. We believe that each person is motivated differently. Sure, there are commonalities, but as you look at the details of how a person accomplishes things, then the uniqueness of what motivates that person emerges.

In order to describe the phenomena that we see, we have broken our observations into five pieces which together form an individual's MAP. These are not types, just categories that allow us to organize and better articulate the observations we make as we review the data from the SIMA achievement interview.

Another way to explain these five categories is to use the analogy of describing someone physically. If I were to do so, I might say, "Here's what the head looks like," and describe what I see; "Here's the shape of the torso," and describe it—down to the legs and feet. So, just as someone can be described physically, we can, through the MAP, describe one's unique pattern of motivation. The five categories that make up a Motivated Abilities Pattern are:

- Circumstances or Conditions within which the individual is motivated to work

- Subject Matter the individual is motivated to work with or through

- Abilities the individual is motivated to use

- Operating Relationship the individual strives to establish with others

- The overall Central Motivational Theme that drives the individual

The value of understanding Motivational Patterns is that very practical questions regarding best use of a person can be answered. Some of these questions are:

- Will this person be most effective working as part of a team or independent of one?

- Will this person thrive within an entrepreneurial work environment?

- Will this person be effective in taking an idea and building upon it?

- How much definition and structure does this person need in order to be most effective?

- Will this person be effective in opening up a new market?

- Is this individual better at creating from scratch or developing from something that exists or in implementing something after it is developed?

- How motivated will this person be to achieve the objectives within deadlines?

- Should I assign this person the task of checking the details?

When you understand the Motivational Patterns of people, you will be able to make better decisions about them. For example, if you look at the Subject Matter that a person is motivated to work with, you might see that he or she is motivated by ideas and concepts and not details; or by technology and not people; or by tools and not information—and, as a result, make a more informed decision about how to most effectively use that person's talents.

Similarly, when you understand the Abilities that a person is motivated to use, you will have a better understanding of whether or not that individual will be effective at certain tasks; for example, probing to get to the bottom of things or convincing people to participate or laying out the procedures to be followed.

When you understand the Circumstances or Conditions that motivate a person to perform at his or her best, you can better predict whether or not the work environment will enhance success. For example, does it have a lot of uncertainty versus following a routine—or is there a lot of opportunity for visibility versus being behind the scenes—or does the culture support quick decisions and taking action versus a well-thought-out, methodical approach?

When you understand the type of Relationship to others a person prefers to establish, you can better assess the chances of success when making assignments. For example, will this person be effective in a role where he or she needs to spark others or to do a lot of detailed oversight or to work alone and take care of all the details.

When you understand the Central Motivational Theme of a person, you have a greater chance to determine whether or not the nature of the assignment aligns well with the basic nature of the individual. For example, will this person be effective in a turnaround situation where there are overwhelming problems (is this individual motivated by turnarounds and problems?), or in opening foreign markets (is this individual motivated to establish something new and to deal with different cultures?), or in exploiting a product's potential (does he or she have an exploitive nature?)?

When people work in situations that "fit" with their Motivational Patterns, they have a greater chance to realize personal success. When the work is opposite the Motivational Pattern, then the chances of frustration and failure are almost certain.

On the following pages, each of the five categories of the MAP will be described in greater depth. I am describing this to you to enrich your understanding as to how they function and can be identified. Through these five ingredients, a picture can be drawn of a person in action, when he or she is most highly motivated.

As you begin to understand the ingredients that make up Motivational Patterns, you will improve your ability to recognize them and make more effective managerial decisions regarding your life and the lives of people for whom you have responsibility.

Before we look at each category, let me emphasize that a MAP is an integrated system. What I mean by that is that each piece is best understood in light of the other pieces. For example, each of us is motivated to use certain Abilities. This doesn't mean that we can't use other Abilities, but there are some that we are naturally drawn toward using. And we each like to use those Abilities on certain Subject Matter. This doesn't mean that we can't work with other Subject Matter, but when we can use our Motivated Abilities on Subject Matter that is motivating to us, then we have a greater chance to function at our best.

Each of us also has conditions under which we like to work. This doesn't mean that we can't work under other conditions, but when we can use our Motivated Abilities on our motivated Subject Matter within our motivated Circumstances or Conditions, then we are likely to be more highly motivated. And when we can do this and establish the type of Relationship to others that we prefer, then we increase our chances for success.

When the overall focus of the work fits, not only the Abilities, Subject Matter, Conditions, and Relationship, but also the Central Theme, then this is when we are at our highest level of motivation and most likely to be our most effective.

Working Within Certain Circumstances

The first piece of the MAP that I would like to describe in greater detail involves the Circumstances or Conditions within which people are motivated to operate. Each of us have situations that trigger and sustain our interest—sort of the spark that ignites the fire and the fuel that keeps it going.

One type of Circumstance is a triggering mechanism. For example, consider the person who loves to solve problems who arrives at work to find something is not working. If the Subject Matter fits and other aspects of the Motivational Pattern can be engaged, then this person is drawn to the situation—like a magnet drawing metal toward it.

Another type of Circumstance is one that sustains a person's motivation. How motivated would you be if you thrived on working alone but worked in an environment where everything was always done by committee; or you were motivated to follow precise techniques and you were handed a hastily and sloppily prepared manual to follow? Let us look at a few examples of Circumstances from the MAPs of other people:

Audiences/Viewers	New
Deadlines	Problems
From Scratch	Requirements
Lack of Pressure	Scripted Situations
Need for Accuracy	Support Role
Need for Efficiency	Unstructured Situations

Circumstances often pull us in, keep us motivationally going, and often determine in which direction we will proceed. For example, the salesperson, teacher, or engineer who is motivated to exploit potential will always be looking at what is possible. The person motivated to work on projects will be attracted to activity that has a beginning and end and will try to handle work like a project or a series or projects. People who like competition will come alive when they compete and will not perform as well when the sense of competition is removed. The person drawn to needs and causes will respond when they emerge.

To determine which Circumstances exist within a Motivational Pattern, we look for enough evidence to suggest its importance to the individual. This doesn't mean that a Circumstance needs to be evident in every achievement, but it does mean that it needs to be in enough of them to demonstrate its motivational importance.

What follow are two examples from people who were interviewed. This first example is from a person who enjoys being part of a group or team.

"Grew up on a farm—no friends around—made up several imaginary friends—the animals became my soldiers . . . played football—just being part of the team . . . formed a study group . . . became part of a project team where we all had to . . . my wife and I are a unit . . . pulled people in and got them to work together."

In this second example, you will read excerpts from the achievements of a person who enjoys precision and accuracy.

"Built models, concentrated on the details to get them perfectly right . . . first place in the science fair with a replica of an irrigation system—worked day and night to get it to come out just right . . . liked working on contracts going over the documents to make sure that each word was absolutely correct—that nothing was left out or wrong . . . negotiated the deal down to the last detail—kept everyone there until it was all worked out—didn't want any mistakes . . . redid my kitchen, taking measurements lining up the cabinets, it came out just the way I wanted it to—no mistakes, perfectly lined up."

Each of us has different Circumstances or Conditions that we prefer to operate within. When these conditions are right, we have a greater chance of finding success and satisfaction, to be productive, and to develop the gifts we have been given. When you understand the conditions which motivate or demotivate your employees, your ability to manage will considerably improve.

Working With Certain Subject Matter

The second part of the MAP concerns the Subject Matter to which a person is naturally drawn. We are not saying that people can't work with any Subject Matter—what we are saying is that certain Subject Matter is of a lot more interest to each of us than other Subject Matter and that this has implications regarding our success and satisfaction.

Consider, for example, a person who is motivated to work alone with technology and plans who puts together a great proposal and is then asked to lead the effort to influence various groups to pass the proposal. What starts out as satisfying (working with technology and plans) turns to agony as the job requires working with people and, perhaps, organizational politics.

In this next example, consider what happens to the person who is motivated by details and particulars when invited to participate in a brainstorming session where everyone is dealing with ideas and concepts. If this person is very strong willed, perhaps he or she may try to focus the group to accommodate his or her motivational interests. Regardless of what he or she might do, this individual is likely to experience a disconnect and feel a bit out of place. Frustration abounds when people are asked to work with Subject Matter that is not part of their MAPs. Some examples of Subject Matter are:

Cultures	Procedures/Methods
Details/Particulars	Strategies
Human Behavior	Systems
Ideas/Theories	Techniques
Machinery/Equipment	Visual
Policies	Words/Language

What follow are two examples to illustrate how motivated Subject Matter can be found in an individual's achievements. As with Circumstances, a particular Subject Matter doesn't need to appear in every achievement to be considered part of one's MAP, but it does need to be found in enough of them. The first example is from a person who is motivated to work with ideas.

"We discussed the various ideas that emerged in the group . . . College was fascinating being exposed to all of this new thinking—I just wanted to absorb it all . . . Asked to think of ways to promote the product—was up all night, had so many thoughts— I overwhelmed them the next day . . . Like to keep a journal of my observations—go back and read it periodically, get lost in thought, but it usually leads to something new, a new idea or direction to pursue . . . Like it when I brainstorm with people I work with—always amazed to see how much we come out with."

This next person is motivated to work with living things.

"Nursed the bird back to health . . . grooming the horse—becoming as one when I rode with him . . . trained my dog . . . fed the squirrels . . . built a large bird feeder . . . opened a pet store."

If you understand the Subject Matter that is motivating for you and your employees to work with, it will be more clear as to why, in some cases, there is eagerness and excitement and, in others, eyes glaze over.

Using Certain Abilities

The third part of the MAP describes the Abilities a person is highly motivated to use. These are Abilities the person derives tremendous satisfaction from using; Abilities a person tries to use whenever possible. There are other Abilities that all people have that can be drawn upon, but they are not motivated ones. We call these "can do" skills. When we use our Motivated Abilities, we become absorbed and engaged. We have repeatedly seen that when people excel it is usually when they are using Abilities that are part of their MAP. A few examples of such Abilities from the MAPs of others include:

Adapt/Modify
Analyze/Dissect
Arrange Details/Schedule
Assemble/Fabricate
Build Relationships
Carry Out Directions/Implement
Conceive/Originate
Convince/Persuade
Counsel/Advise
Explain
Give Presentations/Speeches
Grow/Cultivate

Listen/Express
Maintain/Keep in Condition
Manipulate/Subtly Control
Monitor/Make Sure
Nurse/Care For
Plan
Strategize/Chart a Course
Structure/Provide Definition
Suggest/Initiate
Systematize/Proceduralize
Visualize/Picture
Write

People seek to use those Abilities that are part of their MAP and will even perceive what needs doing to be able to do so. We see this all of the time. Watch people and see how they deal with similar situations. The analytical person will seek to pull things apart and examine from various angles; the person who enjoys planning and organizing will seek to put in place an orderly structure to follow; the person who enjoys influencing will seek a way to do so, and so on. If someone is motivated to maintain an ongoing operation, don't expect that individual to drive a lot of changes. Similarly, if one is motivated to change things, don't expect him or her to be very interested in maintaining what exists.

Let's look at two illustrations that will give you an appreciation of how Motivated Abilities are revealed in a person's achievements. The first is from an individual who is motivated to observe detail—*detail* is the Subject Matter, and *observe* is the Ability.

> "Hunted—good at tracking—following the path—partial foot-print, bent or broken branch . . . walked the point in Vietnam—watched the leaves, listened, felt the air, it was like everything was heightened . . . examined the pieces and saw how it worked . . . operated a drill rig—watched what those guys were doing—making sure they didn't make a mistake . . . saw him pack the parachute—noticed that he made a mistake."

In the next illustration, you will see a person who enjoys building and developing things.

> "Built forts . . . creating a ride by hooking up a pulley system to the tree—building this thing was fun . . . made a book shelf in shop class . . . helped my dad build an addition to the house . . . took up bodybuilding—seeing the progress—building myself up . . . becoming an expert—developing my knowledge . . . changed careers—started a wine business—learning all about wines—learning how to run a business—expanding the store."

When we speak of Abilities that are motivated, we are not talking about things one can do. We are talking about the things one likes to do—enjoys doing—seeks to do and derives satisfaction from doing. These are Abilities that come so naturally that a person probably doesn't even think about them—Abilities that others might immediately mention if asked to describe what someone (who they know well) is good at. When your employees are engaged in work that allows them to use their Motivated Abilities, they not only have a greater chance to be more productive and successful, but they have a greater chance to feel satisfied and good about what they are doing. This is true not only for your employees but for yourself as well.

Operating Relationship With People

The fourth piece of the MAP is how one is motivated to operate or interact with others. For example, some people prefer to be part of a group, while others prefer to do things alone. Some people like to initiate or spark, while others prefer being a steady influence. Some like coaching, some directing, others overseeing.

The following are a few examples of ways people operate that will provide you with an understanding of this important ingredient to the MAP:

Participant   Wants to share in an effort with others.

Key Resource   Enjoys filling a key role whose contribution is critical to the success.

Spearhead   Wants to be the person who generates momentum for a new activity.

Director   Wants others to do things exactly the way he wants.

Team Leader   Participates with subordinates in the action—leads by example.

Coach   Wants to develop the capability of others.

Liaison   Enjoys serving as a connecting link.

It is difficult for some people not to seek a role where they are attempting to have significant influence just as it is painful for others to have the burden of making sure people do their work. There are many different ways of interacting with others, but only some of them are highly motivating. Let us now look at the words of an individual who enjoys overseeing or making sure work gets done.

> "Always got good grades in school—always did my assignments, did them well and got them in when due . . . ran the school store—made the work schedule—ordered the merchandise—kept the books . . . kept track of everyone's credits—let people know where they stood . . . ran the sorority house—kept the books— hired the cook—maintained order—organized clean-up—made sure that people followed through . . . monitored what the groups did—let them know when they fell behind . . . put a system in place to track production . . . went to Mexico to make sure it was being done right."

In this next illustration, are the words of a person who likes to get things started but prefers not to have any sustaining involvement once that which he starts is set in motion.

> "It was my idea that we form our own club—not much else after that—just one of the guys . . . wrote an article for the school newspaper that created an uproar . . . just stood up and told everyone why I thought we should do it—got it all going . . . came up with this creative idea which the team used . . . listening to them and giving them suggestions—love it when they try it and it works."

When you get into the details and intricacies of the Relationship aspects of a person's MAP, then much can be explained. Why, for example, people are attracted to each other—why they avoid certain situations and are drawn to others—why one boss micromanages while another is very hands-off—why one boss steps into his employees' work at certain times but ignores what they do at other times.

When you have a better understanding of the preferred Relationships of your employees, then decision making and managing their success and productivity become easier. Similarly, the same is true for you.

Central Motivational Theme

The final ingredient is the Central Motivational Theme. It is the most important and revealing aspect of one's MAP. You will find it in every one of an individual's achievements. It is always present. You should see clear evidence of it in all of a person's achievements. In many ways it is like finding a theme to a poem, in that one needs to dig deep to see the common thread within each achievement. Let us look at a few examples of Central Motivational Themes:

Acquire/Possess	Improve/Make Better
Be in Charge/In Control	Make the Team/Grade
Comprehend and Demonstrate	Master/Perfect
Develop/Build/Form	Maximize/Make the Most Of
Excel/Be the Best	Meet Requirements/Specifications
Extract Potential	Overcome/Prevail
Gain Response/Influence Behavior	Pioneer/Explore

Every achievement that one has that he or she enjoys doing and believes was done well will allow his or her Central Theme to be accommodated. By examining the details of a person's achievements, you should be able to see his or her Theme emerge. At People Management, we do not have a set number of Central Themes. The words selected are used to capture the essence of the person and the Central Theme that emerges for that individual.

As an illustration, the following achievements are from a person who enjoys realizing a concept. This person sees things in her mind's eye and moves toward making what is seen happen.

> "Even though I was a girl, my dad wanted a son—an athlete he could be proud of—I used to watch the games on television and visualize how to play the game—I'd work at it and practice until I could play the way I wanted."

> "Enjoyed putting together the yearbook—laying out the photographs—had an image of what I wanted—moved photos around until it came out right—the way I wanted it to be—when it was all done, I was proud of the way it looked."

"Became a big sister—saw what she could accomplish—kept talking to her about the future and what she could be—what she could achieve—finally got her to believe—to see what I saw—coached, guided, and counseled her—she has become the woman I knew she could be."

"Designed my own home—started with an idea and fleshed it out—looked at floor designs—bought a computer program that allowed me to play around with ideas—once it was set, went to an architect—worked with him to be sure it could be done—hired a contractor—was there every day making sure they were doing things right."

In order for satisfaction to be obtained, the Central Theme must be accommodated—it must be allowed to express itself. If it can't, then frustration sets in and one's motivational drive is drained.

Imagine for a moment that this person who is motivated to realize concepts, ends up working for a boss who enjoys initiating new directions, and frequently pulls people off of assignments in order to mobilize around new thrusts. How frustrating it would be for this individual to formulate the image, begin to move toward it, but not be allowed to bring it to realization.

In this second example, you will see the Central Theme of a person who is motivated to explore. You will see how the process of learning, discovery, and exploration dominates and drives this individual.

"Used to get on my bike early in the morning and rode into new parts of town and just see things."

"Decided to go to college in Boston which was 3,000 miles from my home—just felt it was the place to go—the city was so alive—so much to see—so much to do."

"Got curious as to how the machine worked—looked at it—fixed it—fun to reconfigure it in such a way that we got more production out of it—incorporated some of the new stuff into it—got lost in learning all about it."

"Taking my kids on little adventures—once we spent an entire day trying to find a secluded pond—got lost—exciting though—seeing things along the way—trying to figure out where we were—kids loved it—we all got caught up in the excitement—just seeing all the beauty around us and being part of it and sharing it with my kids—proud that I was able to give them that type of experience."

This person will flourish in roles where one can be paid to roam and learn and will die a slow death in a role that requires doing the same thing over and over, day in and day out.

Once you understand the Central Themes in the lives of your employees and yourself, it will be easier to select paths to success. You will find that when a person's Central Theme is fully engaged, the person will feel success and satisfaction—a source of great joy—and when it cannot be expressed, you will find that your employees (and you) will feel frustrated and unfulfilled. And if you feel that way, it is difficult to sustain effectiveness.

Putting It All Together

There are many different ways that Motivational Patterns can be presented. In most situations, we write commentary that describes the person's MAP. This commentary can be a few pages or many. In most of the reports that we write, we also include an outline of the individual's MAP. The outline contains words that reflect the person's Motivational Pattern and is arranged in such a way that a reader can look at it and gain a clearer picture of the individual and how he or she is motivated to perform his or her best. What follows is an example of what a Motivated Abilities Pattern outline looks like. MAP outlines can be difficult to work with at first, but if you spend time examining the words, you can learn much about an individual. So, I ask you to spend a few minutes with the one that follows. To assist you, let me mention that this person is a president of a company. As you look at his MAP outline, ask yourself the following:

- If this person were managing your company, where is he likely to focus his energies?

- When is this person likely to become most energized?

- What aspects of running a business are likely to be frustrating for this person to deal with?

- What types of people would this person work most and least effectively with?

- What aspects of the job is this person likely to be most and least effective in doing; i.e., finance, marketing, sales, manufacturing, product development, working with customers, motivating employees, handling crises, making deals, handling logistics, setting up systems, helping people, etc.

- If you were an investor in this company, what might make you nervous (given this president's Motivational Pattern)?

- If this person is successful as a president, what are likely to be the reasons?

- If this person fails as president, what are likely to be the reasons?

- If you owned the company, what actions could you take to enable this president to be more successful?

MAP Outline of a Company President

What is the Central Motivational Theme of this person?

To explore, extract, and maximize potential

- For profit, reaction, influence, understanding, reputation, uniqueness, perfection

- While maintaining pace, action, movement, excitement, centrality, "on the run" involvement

What Circumstances trigger this person's motivation?

Opportunities, Openings
Potential, Possible (rather than known, sure)
Needs, Opportunity to influence people
Emergencies, Crises, Tests, Challenges, Profit potential

What Circumstances sustain this person's motivation?

Opportunity to establish reputation, uniqueness
Open, unstructured, sometimes chaotic setting which requires a
 dynamic response
Variety of tasks
Working from existing ideas and processes
Need for cost wisdom, value consciousness
Competitive environment

What Subject Matter does this individual prefer to work with?

Knowledge, Strategic understanding, Insights, Ideas
Policies, Issues, Concepts
People/Human Behavior
Strategies, Tactics, Angles
Details, Particulars
Personal Expertise

How is this person motivated to Get Information, Expertise, or Knowledge?

Learning:
> *by listening, expressing*

Investigating:
> *by surveying, gathering information, inquiring, extracting, exploring, reading*

How is this person motivated to Evaluate or Process Information?

Evaluating:
> *by figuring, calculating/assessing, interpreting, deciphering/ conceptualizing*

How is this person motivated to Organize and Plan?

Organizing:
> *by integrating, gathering pieces together, categorizing*

How is this person motivated to Develop, Create, Produce, and Do the Work?

Doing:
> *by doing physically, manually*

Developing:
> *by synthesizing, blending, adapting, formulating/refining, shaping, building relationships*

How is this person motivated to Influence, Manage, and Communicate?

Influencing:
> *by initiating, suggesting, involving, gaining participation, motivating, advising, deal-making*

Teaching:
  by coaching, stimulating, demonstrating

Communicating:
  by conferring, discussing, writing

How does this person Work Best With People?

Key Contributor (Individualistic)
Coaching Sparkplug and Initiator/Organizer

What are some of the important Results this person is motivated to work toward?

Response, Impact on People
Uniqueness/Reputation
Profit

To assist you in understanding this person and in answering the questions I posed, I am going to make some observations about this individual's Motivational Pattern in order to jump-start your thinking process.

- Enjoys roaming and exploring and extracting that which has potential

- Needs to be involved in activities that are intense

- Subject Matter tends to focus on ideas, concepts, strategies, people, etc., but not on other things like technology, finance, operations, systems

- Has a nose for how to make money

- Attracted to opportunities where he can establish himself and his image and reputation and make an impact

- Drawn more toward initiating and sparking, as opposed to following through or ongoing operations

- Good at synthesizing and interpreting

- Good at adapting (himself, others, his organization, plans, policies, strategies)

- Tends to be reactive and spontaneous—formulates strategies on the run—not one to plan and stick to the plan

- Maintaining order, structure or consistency would not be a strength

- Has a large and diverse number of influencing and communication motivations

Having this level of understanding of yourself and those you manage does not guarantee success, and it doesn't even guarantee that you will make the "best" decision. It does, though, provide additional insight that can be factored into decisions.

Now, take a few minutes and review the president's MAP outline, and see what observations you can make. The questions that precede the outline should trigger your thinking. Write your thoughts in the space below.

_____

_____

_____

_____

_____

_____

_____

_____

CHAPTER IV

The Meaning of Your MAP

It is not work that kills men; it is worry. . . .
It is not the revolution that destroys the machinery,
but the friction.

—Beecher

It is important to understand what a MAP is. A person's Motivated Abilities Pattern is not merely a collection of words and phrases or a list of skills and abilities. It is a holistic description of that individual when he or she is motivated to perform at his or her best. Once you understand its dynamics and how to use it, your ability to manage people will significantly improve. As you delve into the truth about people, you will find that knowledge of a person's MAP (and your MAP) can become a valuable tool. But first, I would like for you to understand more fully this phenomenon that exists within all people and some of its implications for you personally and as a manager.

The MAP is Practical

When people are engaged in activity that draws upon their MAPs, they usually perform to the best of their capability. In contrast, when people are involved in activity, paid or otherwise, that is opposite the nature of their MAPs, they inevitably become frustrated and end up performing at levels below what they are capable of. Organizations that recognize this basic principle will improve organizational effectiveness simply by seeking to maximize individual effectiveness.

The MAP is an Integrated System

As previously stated, MAPs have a systemic nature to them. They are most useful when not divided into pieces, when each element is perceived in the context of all the other elements described. As you begin to understand the MAPs within your employees and perhaps your own, it is important to recognize that each element enables, defines, and modifies every other element. In other words, the person seeks to achieve certain Outcomes, using certain Abilities, working through, and with, certain Subject Matter, within certain Circumstances and maintaining certain Operating Relationships to the other parts. For example, an Ability to evaluate by appraising worth, along with other Abilities in the pattern, is applied on the Subject Matter of structural objects, vehicles, groups of people, and money—within Circumstances that involve competition, where an immediate response is required, in a participative environment, working from scratch—in an Operating Relationship where the individual is functioning as a team member—all of which is driven by a Central Motivational Theme of meeting requirements established by others.

The more an entire MAP is engaged, the more highly motivated a person will be. If one or more critical elements of a MAP are not present, then the person is not likely to be highly motivated. In general, if you can match high motivation to organizational need, then you will increase performance. This should be a major goal of all managers of people.

The MAP Emerges Early, Remains Constant, and Seeks Expression

Almost everyone that we, at People Management, interview recalls a first achievement around age five. Some people, though, start earlier. Beginning with the first achievement, the basic structure of one's MAP can be seen. As people describe the achievements that range over their lives, their MAPs mature, become sharper and clearer, but their essence doesn't change.

There is no doubt that life experiences, including more sophisticated or complex achievement experiences, have an impact on people, but we have also seen that the essential nature of one's MAP remains constant. We have seen this regardless of environment, education, changes in values, exposure to new philosophies, tragedies, or defining moments. MAPs have an inherent nature to them. They seek expression and will attempt to find ways to emerge—in spite of their surroundings. MAPs are like meandering rivers that seek their natural course. The exploiter of potential will always be looking for gold nuggets, the nurturer for something to take care of, the risk taker for something that has an element of danger, the pioneer for a new frontier to explore.

We are not saying that what people experience in life does not have an impact—it obviously does. Life experiences do have a significant influence on direction, values, where one's gifts are applied, and even on the level and intensity of achievements and the quality of life. But what we have repeatedly seen is that MAPs remain constant in spite of the richness or austerity of the environment.

The environment can help to bring out and develop the MAP or it can inhibit its growth. For example, the person motivated to overcome obstacles who thrives on challenges is almost always stimulated by poverty, handicaps, or circumstances that may cause others to give up. The individual gifted with extraordinary eye-hand coordination, born to a family that does not value education or even training, may grow to be effective at fixing things but not a highly-skilled surgeon or craftsman.

We are not saying that people don't change. People do learn, grow, and develop within the nature of their MAPs, but the essence of their Motivational Patterns remains consistent. The environment may help determine exactly where one's MAP gets applied, to what degree, and at what level; but the fundamental nature of the MAP is not changed— shaped, yes, but not changed.

As a manager of people, it can be quite valuable to understand and accept this principle and to use it as a guide as you evaluate people and situations and make decisions about utilization.

We Perceive Through the Eyes of Our MAP

We have seen, in our consulting with individuals, that people often perceive situations and what they feel is required through the eyes of their MAPs. Look, for example, where those who lead businesses focus. Where one takes over an organization and says, "We need to increase our marketing efforts," another executive, in the same company, feels that the answer lies in greater control. Where one executive looks at a situation and sees the need for great change, another sees the need to strengthen what already exists. Some people drive diversification or acquisition, while others consolidation.

We frequently see, when conducting achievement interviews with executives and developing their MAPs, that company direction and decisions are a reflection of the executive's Motivational Pattern—whether it be a focus on new product introductions, quality, service, the education and development of employees, being the dominant player, finding the market niche, following a detailed plan, remaining flexible and open to opportunity, leading the pack, counterpunching, creating value where there is little, doing extensive due diligence, or going on gut and instinct.

The implications of this are not insignificant. We all tend to see the world through our MAPs. If people are not aware of their MAPs and the influence on perception, then the MAPs will tend to control them, rather than their being in control.

For example, if you are motivated to experiment and try things, and your boss is motivated to plan, define structure and carry out, you can anticipate where the natural areas of conflict are likely to emerge as decisions are made as to the management of people, where resources are placed, and how the organization should evolve.

If situations are so clear, why do all people not perceive things the same way? How can ten people have the same experience, see the same thing, or hear the same words, but differ on what they later describe?

You can help people to better understand their Motivated Patterns and the implications of how they naturally seek to accomplish things. You can even teach them to recognize when their MAPs do not serve them well and to find ways to modify their behavior. But the essence of who they are remains consistent, and without understanding their inherent nature, people will perceive what needs to be focused on and done in accordance with their Motivational Patterns—whenever possible.

Look at how people in similar jobs do those jobs differently. One person is very neat and organized, another is spontaneous and chaotic. One focuses on concepts and ideas, while another focuses on details and technique. When given the chance, people will try to perform jobs to accommodate their MAPs.

Once you understand and accept that all people see the world through the eyes of their MAPs (including you), then you can make more effective life, work, and day-to-day decisions. Once you recognize this, then you can improve relationships with those with whom you work and live. You can improve your performance or the performance of those for whom you have responsibility.

Once you understand and accept this, then you can become more aware of why you (and others) decide as you do. With this awareness you might elect to make different decisions or consciously stay the course.

When you set direction, establish policies, choose strategies, or implement to accommodate your MAP, but are not aware of how your MAP affects your perception, then you are at a disadvantage. The ability to step back and evaluate with this knowledge will enable you to be a more effective leader and manager. Likewise, when you can help others to evaluate their decisions and actions, then you are adding value to your organization and to your employees.

Many years ago, I met a corporate head of technology who had responsibility for an extensive research organization, little of which reported directly to him; most reported up through divisional lines. As the senior vice president of technology, he required all technologists within the research organization, regardless of managerial level (including himself), to spend time at the bench doing hands-on research. When asked why, he stated, "How can one manage researchers if they drift away from doing research?"

In the course of my consulting with this organization, we developed his MAP and saw that his primary learning mechanism was to have a direct, hands-on involvement. I pointed out to him that his policy, which operated for a number of years, was a reflection of his own learning style. As I pointed this out, he leaned back in his chair and smiled. The policy didn't change, but he wasn't quite as insistent that everyone spend time at the bench doing research.

Organizations, in their desire to operate more effectively, can create a culture that reinforces the awareness of MAPs and how they impact decisions and actions. For example, one of our clients, a service company, has made extensive use of SIMA, and the leaders and managers of the organization share the results of their MAPs openly with each other. When disagreements emerge or strategies formulated or tactics chosen or people selected or teams formed or needs identified or people evaluated, the knowledge of individual MAPs is continually factored in. There is an openness and receptivity that exists that results in people accepting the nature of their Motivational Patterns and the inherent positives and negatives. Rather than argue and defend, people accept and understand (as best they can). Rather than seeing political agendas, people understand that it's easy to project the worst onto others.

It is difficult for organizations to reach this level of trust and open-ness, but it starts at the top, with a leader who is willing to let others understand his or her strengths and potential areas of weakness. It takes tremendous courage to be open about your imperfections, but when you do, it helps to establish a culture where the entire body is striving to work as one as opposed to a lot of individual parts, each striving to accomplish things, but not always the same things—two steps forward, one step back, one-half step sideways.

Meaning and Satisfaction Comes From Using Your Map

People range over their lifetimes and select achievements that they "enjoyed doing" and "felt that they did well." These are achievements from which they derive great satisfaction. The SIMA process and MAP product are merely mechanisms we use to organize and describe these themes that exist within all people.

It is true that the MAP tends to lead a person and will look for ways to express itself, but when it is thwarted and held in check, then people tend to find that life has less meaning for them. In contrast, when the MAP fits and is allowed to fully express itself, then the person feels ener-gized and alive.

When I first met him, he had just been promoted to general manager with a big raise—could life be any better? He had done so well estab-lishing the structure, setting up the business and working through the strategies. He was a young MBA who was moving ahead quickly and his bosses saw his talent and rewarded his success by giving him a business to run. Two years later, when I met him again, he looked terrible. His appearance and the aura around him told anyone with any degree of sen-sitivity that something was wrong. I gently probed. It didn't take much for all of his misery and self-doubt to pour out. He felt trapped in a job that had little meaning and satisfaction for him, and he was paying a price. As we spoke, it was clear to me that he was motivated to establish a business, not to run one—that he was motivated to do the work himself, not to accomplish it through others. As he grew the business, dealing with the "every day" and all of the delegation or non-delegation, it was killing him (literally).

He was determined to continue his path to success. He just kept disciplining himself to do what needed to be done. He didn't complain and told everyone that all was well. People could see that something was wrong, but financial results were good.

He went through the SIMA process (for his eyes only). He understood why the role he was in didn't fit, but he was determined, despite my counseling, to persevere. He was determined to stay and continue to show all how good he was. He was age 38 when he had a heart attack.

Lots of other things can have a bearing on satisfaction and happiness: relationships, money, living conditions, expectations, injuries, appearance, chemical imbalance, among others; but one critical factor is whether or not the Motivational Pattern is being engaged.

Even if all other conditions are positive, if a person's MAP is not being used appropriately, then that person will not feel the level of satisfaction and fulfillment that could be felt.

A Word About Incentives and Rewards

To encourage the individual, you must understand what that person holds dear. The overuse of money, status, and power as the "carrots" for most people have some, but usually not, sustaining value, unless those elements are part of one's MAP. Once those things are obtained, people look for more. Just look around and see the people who have left good-paying, high-status jobs for something else that pays less or has less prestige. The executive who goes into classroom teaching, the CPA/CFO who resigns to open a retail business, the advertising executive who moves out of the city into the country to open an antique shop are but a few examples of people whom I have met.

I am not saying that paying well does not motivate people. But it is a temporary fix for most. Certainly if people feel underpaid it will have a negative effect, and the same can be said for not being promoted to the level and title to which one aspires.

As an executive recruiter, I have learned that when prospects raise their hands to be considered as candidates for positions, the reason frequently has to do with their not feeling highly motivated by their work. Sometimes, candidates seek to change positions because they just want to change what they are doing. Sometimes the opportunity that is being presented sounds too attractive to pass up (taps into the heart of their motivation)—so they listen and consider.

I have found that when the reason for change is financial, then it becomes more difficult to recruit people because all the person's immediate employer needs to do to retain the employee is to increase his or her compensation.

The lesson here for managers of people is not only to pay their employees well, but more importantly, to understand what the motivational drivers are for each and to work hard at trying to put people into roles that allow them to use their MAPs.

The cost of not doing this is high—not only in terms of lost potential of people and what they can accomplish and the rippling effect it has on others and within the organization, but also in saving on replacement costs.

What most people really want is the opportunity to perform work that engages their MAPs—to be hooked into activity that continually reinforces the core of who they are—that hits them at a level which no amount of money, power, or status can. Money can provide a degree of freedom, but it can't create work satisfaction or produce a highly-motivated person.

The MAP Explains Behavior

Once you read the MAPs of people, it is easy to see why they behave and perform as they do. So often people finger point and blame and not truly understand. For example, one illustration of this that I encountered early in my consulting involved a researcher who was motivated to pioneer, innovate, initiate, and drive things to completion who was assigned to a technical manager who was motivated to keep an operation running smoothly. As I provided consultation to the vice president of research, he told me that the subordinate complained to him that his boss was "old thinking, blocking progress, and will eventually be the ruination of the department," and that the department head came to him and said, "I need to terminate this subordinate because he is disrupting the entire department."

The ability to examine a situation and explain it has proved repeatedly helpful in our consulting with individuals and organizations; e.g., why someone insists on getting into every detail, doesn't tie up loose ends, is great with customers but a bear internally, excellent as a project leader but not very good as a day-to-day manager, etc.

Motivated vs. Unmotivated Behavior

When people are engaged in unmotivated activity, they sometimes exhibit different behavior from that which they display when they are doing what has motivating value to them. The essential difference between the two is that in motivated behavior, the person's giftedness is engaged, whereas in unmotivated behavior, one's MAP is not engaged. The failure to consider this difference has, in our opinion, led to observations which do not distinguish between motivated behavior and "can do" behavior.

We all have the capacity to grit our teeth and behave a certain way for a period of time. In our experience, "can do" behavior can rarely be sustained on a continual basis for any significant length of time at a high level of performance. Just because one does it once or twice doesn't mean that high productivity will always be forthcoming.

The MAP Needs Discipline and Nurturing

Just because people have been given gifts doesn't mean that they will grow fully. Just because they are gifts doesn't mean that they are always a benefit. In the right place they will enable people to accomplish, but in the wrong context, they can be a detriment. Part of the process of maturing in one's ability to understand and manage oneself is recognizing when one's MAP is a strength or a potential weakness.

Just as people have been given physical bodies to grow, develop, or abuse, so have they been given Motivational Patterns. If people don't exercise them, discipline them, and nurture them—their Patterns won't grow fully. If people allow things to interfere with the development of their MAPs, they will remain stunted—untapped potential.

As people understand the pervasive nature of their Motivated Patterns and face the realities of the world in which we all live, they will be better able to step back and examine performance and behavior. The truth is that people frequently need to temporarily control the pervasive nature of their MAPs in order to best manage situations. MAPs are highly controlling but awareness of their nature enables people to better manage the negative consequences that result when they or one of their employees or peers or charges are in situations that do not accommodate the Motivational Pattern.

For example, the person who is highly motivated to convince and prevail over others needs to learn to moderate his or her behavior in situations that call for listening, patience, and understanding; e.g., as a manager, trying to better understand why the organization is resisting the changes he or she has so persuasively articulated, or perhaps a boss trying to help a highly independent subordinate to learn how to go along.

From a practical perspective, one's MAP is both a strength and a weakness. In the right context it is a strength but, if used uncontrollably, it could be a weakness.

A Phenomenon, Not A Theory

Though there are various theoretical possibilities, we at People Management arc not attempting to explain the reasons for or causes behind one's Motivational Pattern. We make no attempt to get at one's underlying emotional, mental, or attitudinal makeup. We deal with what one has demonstrated, not why.

We also don't consider SIMA a test because there is no measurement against a standard or norm and no comparison to other individuals or groups. Some have verified its effectiveness as a selection tool. Most notable among those who have studied SIMA is the eminent psychologist, Dr. John Crites, who in his evaluative report to his client, McDonnell Douglas Corporation, wrote, "SIMA is both theoretically sound and empirically reliable and valid for use as a selection tool. It meets standards, as enumerated by the American Psychological Association, for the assessment and selection of leaders." He found the profiles to be "stable over time," the level of objectivity to be "outstanding," reliability to be "quite high," and content validity to be "exceptionally high." Overall he found the results to be "unique and highly positive," the findings to be "impressive" and concluded that "SIMA can be used with confidence as a selection and leadership identification method." Others within the testing community (who have examined the validity, reliability, and objectivity of SIMA) see it as an accurate way to measure a person against him or herself over time. A Summary of Research on SIMA can be found in Appendix D.

We see no right or wrong answers and no good or bad responses. What we see and have observed is a phenomenon that every time a person does something he or she enjoys and believes was done well, that person uses some or all of the recurring ingredients of what we call a Motivated Abilities Pattern.

CHAPTER V

Using Your MAP

He is a wise man who wastes no energy on the pursuits for which he is not fitted.

–Gladstone

To be successful in life is not an easy matter. Many people survive and can even point to successes they have had. But how often does a person, in the larger context, feel that his or her life was successful?

In measuring success, people often start by looking at where they end up on the finish line or where they are in the race. Success, though, can't be measured in such a way.

Many of us will reach a point where we measure success by looking at moments—situations in our lives where we made decisions and acted on them. And if the decisions we made and actions took reinforced the positive nature and strength within us, then our self-assessments will be positive. But if we have made decisions and taken actions that, in hindsight, move us away from positive feelings about ourselves, then there is disappointment and a sense that more could have (and perhaps should have) been achieved—that our lives were not successful.

The lives we lead are filled with choices, and it is the sum total of those choices that add up to feelings of success or failure. When you take on the responsibility of managing people, you take on a responsibility to assist them in their pursuit of success. We all have responsibility for our own success, but the manager, by virtue of the relationship, has a degree of responsibility for others—it goes with the turf. By understanding the nature, dynamics, and implications of MAPs you can make better managerial decisions regarding your employees, organizations and yourself.

At times it is good to have a strong will, but it can also result in your being a lonely person. At times it is good to be highly gifted in influencing people, but it can also corrupt the soul when turned inward to be completely self-serving. At times it is great to be drawn to the new, but it can be sad when there is nothing permanent and sustained as a result.

Through the eyes of our MAPs we see the world around us and through those eyes, we make decisions. Knowing your MAP and learning how to use it to better evaluate situations and make decisions will enable you to be a better manager of yourself. As you become a better manager of yourself, you will become a better manager of others.

In this chapter, I will explore ways that people have applied knowledge of their MAPs to real life situations. My intent here is to give you ideas as to how you can apply the knowledge of your MAP in several critical areas of your life. The areas that we will look at are:

- Improving performance (yours as well as your organization's).
- Improving job fit, work satisfaction, and career decision making.
- Enhancing the learning process.
- Enhancing relationships.

Improving Performance

Later on I will share some of my thoughts about how to take what you have learned about yourself and your MAP and to use that awareness as a beacon to help you find work that could give you that feeling of fulfillment. What I am going to delve into here is how organizations (enlightened ones, I like to think) have used Motivational Patterning in the work setting.

In broad terms, we have applied MAPs and the SIMA technology in:

- Selection (hiring, promotion, succession).
- Enhancing individual and organizational effectiveness.
- Helping to resolve conflict or performance problems.
- Helping teams function more effectively.
- Providing guidance when issues of job fit arise.

Making Better Selection Decisions

Perhaps one of the most important functions of management, in any organization, is determining who gets a job. Make good selection decisions and your chances of success are greatly enhanced. Make poor selection decisions and your chances of success are not very good.

When you look to fill a job and a candidate is in front of you, there are, in broad terms, three things to look at. First is the candidate's background and experience. Does this person have the right kinds of experience necessary to do the job well? Second is, can I get along with this person, and will he or she go about doing the job and interacting with me and others in a way that gives me comfort and confidence? Third is pure chemistry—will I hit it off with this person?

Managers rarely hire people who have the right background and experience in whom they don't feel comfortable. Managers do, though, frequently hire people who lack some of the desired experience with whom they do feel comfortable.

My point here is that a lot of selection decisions are made every day based upon perceptions of compatibility. Most of these decisions are based upon gut and feel.

Consider the manager who is very organized and stays on top of the details. Would this manager be comfortable with a subordinate who is motivationally interested in expressing ideas and getting things initiated but is only concerned with organization and detail during the start-up phase—even though they hit it off well in the interview? What are the chances of success if the boss is motivated by meeting time deadlines in a concise manner and the subordinate likes to roam, explore, and have a lot of learning time? These are but two examples in an endless sea of issues that can emerge when looking at the simple question of "Will this person do the job well, and can we get along?"

An erroneous assumption made in many selection and promotion decisions is that people adapt to the requirements of a job and, therefore, will perceive and perform the job in terms of an objective analysis of what is needed.

As stated earlier, in our experience at People Management, people tend to perceive and attempt to perform any job in a way which makes use of and can potentially fulfill their Motivational Patterns, and that elements of the job which conflict with a person's MAP will significantly frustrate that person, resulting in poor work performance. We have repeatedly seen that the better the fit between the job and the person's MAP, the better the chance of success.

We believe that before candidates are interviewed, a manager should identify the elements of the job necessary in order for a person to be successful on the job. These elements then constitute the screen or measuring stick to which an individual's MAP can be contrasted. This helps one to look beyond initial impressions and get at the substance of the critical issue of compatibility.

Defining what is needed, apart from the desired background and experience, is best accomplished by asking not only what you want done but also how you want it done. For example, "We want this person to lead the organization in selling $200 million in business"; "How do you want her to accomplish this?" should be the follow-up question. "We want systems put in place that enable us to track progress and performance"; "What is involved in building these systems?" and "What does this person need to do to successfully build them?" should be the follow-up questions. Once you can describe a job in terms of the critical behaviors necessary, then it becomes much easier to select the best candidate. The first step then is to carefully describe a job in as much detail as possible—what you want done and how you want it done.

Now let's look at how you can use SIMA principles to help determine whether or not a candidate is a good fit with a job. As you interview a candidate, try to use what you have learned about SIMA to determine what is in the heart of the candidate. In addition to normal questions you might ask, take a journey into the person's achievements and see what they reveal: For example, you might ask, "I see that you worked at _____ as a _____ , is that a job that you enjoyed?" Assuming that the answer is "yes," then follow up with, "Could you tell me about what you enjoyed about the work, what you found particularly satisfying?"

Asking people to talk about achievements, how they went about accomplishing things and what they found satisfying will be far more revealing than many other kinds of questions—some of which might have little bearing as to how successful one will be once on the job. Questions to understand one's Motivational Pattern (even glimpses of it) help to round out what you need to know about a candidate before a hiring decision should be made.

I am not saying that you don't need to ask questions to determine if candidates have the right background, experience, philosophy, etc., but assuming they do, then how people are motivationally put together, and how they are likely to move once on the job, is valuable insight. Consider the value of hearing the following from two candidates:

> **Candidate One:** "I liked being assigned to a customer (even
> though it only happened a few times) and finding out what they
> wanted and getting it for them. . . . I did this by listening care-
> fully, making suggestions, checking with them frequently. . . . I
> just paid a lot of attention to them."

Now let's look at a second candidate.

> **Candidate Two:** "I liked it when—well, one day they assigned
> me to a customer and I really wanted to make a good impression
> so I figured if I could sell them additional business, then my man-
> ager would take better notice of me. . . . What I did is, I became
> friends (sort of) with one of the technical people and I showed
> him how this new stuff was on the cutting edge. . . . I sensed that
> he was drawn to newer technology and convinced him that this
> was something he needed to learn about."

Both candidates were in their late twenties, both had bachelor's
degrees from good schools, and both had similar work experiences in
inside sales and customer service. So, who would you hire?

Now that you have selected one of these candidates, I would like for
you to recognize two things. First, like most people, you probably intuitively reacted more positively to one versus the other. This tells you
something about your own MAP. Second, if you define what you want
done on the job, and how you want it done, then the decision on who to
hire becomes easier.

Let's say that what is critical for success on this job is introducing a
new product to a reluctant and conservative customer. Who would be a
better candidate? Let's say that what is needed is someone to take care of
a long-term customer who is demanding and unforgiving—where atten-
tiveness is of the utmost importance. Who would be the better candidate?

A few thoughts about succession planning: I was asked to provide
counsel to a CEO of a Fortune 200 company who had just been terminated by the company's board. The assignment involved going over the

CEO's MAP report to assess what went wrong and to determine potential paths for the future.

He was an operations and finance person who had come up through the ranks handling every challenge that was presented to him—"turn this around," "start this up," "organize this effort," "diagnose this problem." No matter what he was asked to do, he accomplished it with great determination, decisiveness, and managerial skill. So why was he sitting before me trying to figure out what had gone wrong?

"Being promoted to CEO was one of the happiest moments of my life," he said. "Being let go, one of the darkest." "But I new that something wasn't right—I felt that I was not as decisive as I should have been." I listened to him deal with the embarrassment and pain and his self-assessment. When he slowed down, I gently helped him to understand the nature of one of his dominant motivational themes—to meet needs and requirements. I helped him to understand why such a powerful and decisive person lost because he and the board didn't understand the potential implications of the decision they made.

Succession planning is critical to the success of any organization. A company needs to know who the best prospects are when filling key positions, particularly in terms of the types of situations in which executives will excel. Failure to prepare for succession needs frequently results in rushed decision-making and a greater risk of job mismatch. On the other hand, employees need to identify their motivated strengths to best determine whether or not a promotional opportunity is indeed a good fit for them.

At People Management, we believe that companies should:

- Examine each job on the succession chart and determine what that position actually requires, what needs to be done, and what leadership and/or managerial style is appropriate.

- Develop information on key employees and make determinations as to the situations in which each person is likely to excel.

- Develop employees based upon their potential so if they are promoted, they will have a greater chance of success. This involves creating a developmental plan that capitalizes upon their motivated strengths.

It is our opinion that succession decisions should not be locked in, but assessed at the moment of need. The process should be fluid, where the key decision-makers within the organization look critically at what needs to be done and define those needs as clearly as possible. Once done, the company should then reach for the right person who best fits the situation.

We feel that good succession should also be predictive. That is, as a result of this appointment, what is likely to happen? What is this person likely to focus upon and what might be the consequences of that focus? Where might that person's strengths become weaknesses, what can be anticipated, and what steps can be taken to better ensure this individual's success and, thus, the organization's success?

Let me now return to the terminated CEO. Because he was so decisive, the board asked him to assume control and to establish the company's agenda. Whereas, in the past, the needs and requirements were clearly stated to him, they were now ambiguous. Where in the past, he moved with managerial leadership to achieve the defined goals, he was not sure exactly how to proceed and what to focus on. Rather than being decisive as all had expected, he looked down into the organization for direction. He asked his employees to identify the needs and requirements to focus on because there was no one above him to do so. As a result, his employees felt that there was little direction from above—that there was no clear agenda upon which to focus.

Facing the reality of what went wrong and its implications was difficult for the CEO. Being at the top in an ambiguous situation was not the best situation for him.

Before I move on, let me restate that the SIMA process enables people and employers to make more informed decisions. I am not saying that risks are removed. Any decision that involves matching people to positions is, to some extent, a gamble. The SIMA process is not perfect, but risks can be minimized, and the chances of making good selection decisions can be improved. The bottom line is that it is in the interest of both organizations and individuals for people to be in jobs that fit and maximize motivated strengths.

The former CEO had several opportunities to select from and elected to accept the one where he was vice chairman and number two in an organization that had a strong visionary leader at the top.

Enhancing Effectiveness

One of the principles that you will see woven throughout this section is that to enhance effectiveness, people should concentrate on developing their strengths and look to minimize their weaknesses. A second principle is that one's MAP tends to rule that person's perceptions and, as a result, often determines behavior. However, if people understand their Motivational Patterns, then they are in better positions to make conscious decisions to behave in certain ways. Rather than just react as one's MAP dictates, people can better control the negative side of their Motivational Patterns.

For example, the person who likes to organize everything in sight can step back and say, "If I do that here, then I could drive the team crazy." The team leader who is motivated to persuade and prevail over others can step back and say, "Let me better control those natural urges and work at being more facilitative."

I am not saying that people can change their basic Motivational Patterns, because I have repeatedly seen in my consulting that MAPs do not change. I am saying that people can temporarily adjust themselves so that they don't end up being their own worst enemy.

Always remember, though, if you or others need to adjust so much that you (or they) are being asked to behave in ways that are against the nature of your MAPs most of the time, then the overall fit is not good, and this has significant implications.

An Example to Illustrate: Years ago I was asked by an executive who had been through the SIMA process to provide counsel to his daughter who was not doing well in her classes. After going through the SIMA process, it was clear that the premed courses that she was taking in college did not play into her motivated strengths. She was motivationally interested in people and helping and also numbers, but not science or technology. When her parents asked that I counsel with her again because her grades had not improved, she told me that she had decided to take three science classes, plus one in sociology and another in psychology as a way to see if we were correct. She learned that she had to work so hard to maintain passing grades in the science courses that her work performance in sociology and psychology suffered.

Our work at People Management with individuals has consistently shown us that when people concentrate on developing their motivated strengths, they normally get more results from their investment. This is not to say that people don't benefit from taking courses or workshops to improve weaknesses. What we are saying is, "Be realistic."

Developing Weaknesses: One theory, so to speak, is to understand where someone has weakness—like taking care of details, being organized, thinking creatively, managing projects, analyzing numbers, selling business, or building relationships with customers, and then to develop those weaknesses so they no longer are weaknesses. This is an interesting challenge because if one is not motivated to do any of these things or any of a thousand other activities, then chances are that person will only become, at best, average at them. So, as a manager of others and yourself, when you look to develop a weakness, you are only likely to make it less of a weakness, not a strength.

Developing Strengths: The second theory, so to speak, is to invest developmental dollars in strengths. Here you are likely to get more mileage out of your investment. If people are motivated to plan, they will excel at planning if they develop that natural talent. If people are creative thinkers, they will be even more creative if they attend workshops on creative thinking. If people are managers of relationships, they will better serve an organization and its employees if they are sent to programs on managing people.

Years ago, I came across the fable entitled, "Fable of the Animal School," which further illustrates the value of developing strengths and not overconcentrating on developing weaknesses or believing that weaknesses can be made into strengths.

Fable of the Animal School

Once upon a time, the animals decided they must do something heroic to meet the problems of "a new world"; so they organized a school. They adopted an activity curriculum consisting of running, climbing, swimming, and flying. And to make it easier to administer, all the animals took all the subjects.

The duck was excellent in swimming, better in fact than his instructor, and made passing grades in flying, but was very poor in running. Because he was poor in running, he had to stay after school and also drop swimming in order to practice running. This was kept up until his web feet were badly worn and he was only average in swimming.

The rabbit started at the top of the class in running, but had a nervous breakdown because of so much make-up work in swimming.

The squirrel was excellent in climbing until he developed frustration in the flying class, where his teacher made him start from the ground up, instead of from the treetop down. He also developed charley horses from overexertion, and then got a "C" in climbing and a "D" in running.

The eagle was a problem child and was disciplined severely. In the climbing class he beat all the others to the top of the tree, but insisted on using his own way to get there.

At the end of the year, an abnormal eel had the highest average and was the valedictorian.

I am not saying that you shouldn't look to improve upon areas and activities where you and your employees have minimal motivational interest. Your expectations, though, need to be realistic. If you or others are not motivated to do something, then your goal as a manager should be to help your employees (and yourself) reach a level of performance and awareness where the activity or function is no longer a weakness or detriment to success. To spend an inordinate amount of time trying to turn a weakness (or area of non- or low-motivational interest) into a strength is not productive because it siphons away energy that could best be used to develop strengths to their fullest. Management guru, Peter Drucker, drives this home when he states that, "Effective management is the productive use of strengths."

Strengths Are Also Weaknesses. I have come to learn over the years that the MAP is truly a gift that, when used properly, brings joy to the person and to those around him or her. I have also seen that the MAP in the wrong context is a weakness. I have already sprinkled a few illustrations of this elsewhere, but now I want to concentrate more fully on this important understanding.

In the course of the day, you and your employees will be asked to do many things—some will call upon your Motivational Patterns, and some won't. In some situations, you and your employees will best be served to behave in ways that are opposite the nature of your MAPs because if you and they don't, then you and they could end up creating more headaches for yourself or others. Let's look at two examples.

The Facilitator

Several years ago, I counseled an executive who was passed over for the next level of management. He was very upset and couldn't understand why. He kept emphasizing that he had great ideas, took care of details, made sure the work got done, was thorough in patiently considering options, and was considered to have excellent people skills. His motivational style was to be more of a facilitator which actually worked well within the team management structure of the organization in which he was a team leader. People liked being on his team (for the most part) and the team's results were generally good. Why was he passed over then?

In talking with him, and subsequently his team members and his bosses, I came to understand that in order to be truly effective at the team leader level and the level above that, facilitating the team's effectiveness was critically important. This he actually did quite well. But also of importance was to recognize when it was time to end discussion and use one's expertise and decision-making skills to bring closure. This he was motivationally uncomfortable with. So when the team wanted to move forward and get past the stalemate, he kept facilitating more discussion. Helping him to understand this was difficult, because first I had to show him that what he perceived as being necessary was colored by his MAP—"I don't bring closure because everyone needs to be on board . . . this is what a team is about." Once he understood how his MAP colored his perception and dictated his behavior, he was then open to my feedback which simply was to better recognize when he needed to step in and decide, even though he was uncomfortable doing so.

The Leader

I am reminded of the leader I once met who very energetically communicated his ideas and got employees excited and fired up. His expectations for action and progress were high. Before I counseled him, he was often disappointed and displayed anger because his staff failed to act in the way he wanted them to. Action took place, but progress was not to his liking. Upon developing his MAP, it was clear that he liked to communicate ideas and concepts and use that communication to generate a vision. His insistence that progress take place communicated that he wanted action to result.

When we developed the Motivational Patterns on his lieutenants, it was apparent that his key direct reports needed more of a detailed understanding of what was expected. Each had difficulty translating what the leader wanted into a concrete vision and plan. So the scenario was always the same. The leader stepped back in to see how progress was going, saw the effort heading in the wrong direction, called people into his office, yelled, ranted and raved, and in his disgust and frustration, communicated more precisely what he wanted. In the process, his behavior resulted in people feeling small and unsure. He also felt he could never really trust his people to come through and, thus, always expected unsatisfactory performance. Once the leader understood and accepted the nature of his MAP and that of his staff, and once his staff understood, then less anger and disappointment resulted. The leader worked diligently at being more precise up front. Key employees didn't feel intimidated asking for clarification and more detail. People accepted each other and understood how their MAPs effected behavior and performance.

There are countless other examples I can point to as illustrations— like the manager who liked a highly structured process who inherited a talented employee who needed freedom of movement; or the boss who was motivated by the need for accuracy and precision who tried to get his staff to perform up to his standards; or the person who liked being part of a team who worked for a boss who favored independence.

A few words to those who do executive coaching: Knowledge of an executive's MAP is helpful to coaches as they work with executives to evaluate behaviors and situations. For example, being able to point out that the motivated strength to delve into detail and to control things is a strength that has enabled success, but it can also be a weakness now that the executive is at a level where he or she needs to delegate and counsel with others as opposed to controlling them. Similarly, executives who are motivated to initiate by coming up with creative ideas benefit from coaches who help them to recognize that their staff likes to take the ideas and make them happen—but that when the ideas come out continually and the staff reacts by starting and stopping and changing direction, then the executive's strengths turn into weaknesses.

Being able to step back and evaluate how a MAP is a strength to be capitalized upon or a weakness to be controlled is perhaps the highest usage level of SIMA. People can be, as stated before, their own worst enemy if they don't grow in their awareness of their MAPs. This is not a one shot "Ah!" but a life-long journey of self-discovery and development.

With this in mind, I am suggesting a few exercises to help start your journey. Assuming of course that you already have your MAP or through this book (Appendix A, "Drawing Your MAP") have developed an approximated one or observations about your own design—then try the following.

Looking At Yourself

Using your MAP as a guide, make a list of potential areas of weakness and sources of frustration for you. To do this, look at the flip side of your motivated strengths. The illustration below should help you to develop your own list. First let's look at a paragraph that summarizes the Motivational Pattern of the president whose MAP outline is found on pages 55-57.

"I am a person who sees potential and opportunity in things, particularly people, ideas and ways to excite people and get things done. I like to promote, sell, initiate, and get things started. I'm very concerned with details and meeting the needs of others, particularly when I can establish my reputation and look good in the eyes of others. I'm good in things such as: sales, coaching, client relations, strategizing, and generating ideas."

Given this individual's MAP, then potential areas of weakness and sources of frustration might be:

- Managing or overseeing in a smooth-functioning operation
- Administrative activities
- People who can't be influenced
- Behind-the-scenes job, someone else is the front person
- Quick and dirty work
- People who resist trying things
- Being held back—not being able to move on ideas and observations
- Working for an organization or representing a product that has a questionable reputation

If you have not yet drawn or obtained your MAP, then make a note to remind yourself to return to this section. If you already have your MAP, then I encourage you to develop your list as illustrated above. Before you move on, also spend time answering these questions.

1. What aspects of my MAP are being used in my current job?

2. What aspects of my current job do not fit my MAP?

3. What specific actions can I take that could enhance job fit, further

develop my motivated strengths and increase my personal effectiveness?

Resolving Conflict or Performance Problems

They sat opposite each other, glaring, not listening, thinking of their next retort, blaming. They left the room each shaking his head, each telling his trusted advisers how wrong the other one was, how stubborn, pigheaded and obtuse—each seeing the situation through his own eyes. In the end, nothing was resolved. No meeting of the minds. Little changed except more anger, mistrust, and misunderstanding.

Rather than be trapped and, to some extent, blinded by your MAP, you can look at conflict or performance problems in a different light. Doing so may be uncomfortable, but unresolved problems with people can make your life miserable.

Understanding Motivational Patterns can shed light on a situation, but it can't guarantee that success will follow. To the manager, resolving conflict or performance problems actually represents opportunities to positively impact productivity and employee work satisfaction.

Through SIMA you can identify a person's MAP (as well as your own) and gain an understanding as to why people behave and perform the way they do and why you do as well. You can use SIMA to step back and more objectively try to understand what is contributing to the problem.

When the problem is related to performance, you can more objectively assess job fit and whether or not your (or the employee's) motivated strengths are being used.

In conflict situations, understanding Motivational Patterns can provide a systematic way of sorting out the cause of conflict and help you and others better understand why you or they feel a certain way. Once Motivational Patterns are understood, it is easier to find common ground upon which a new relationship can be built. Motivational Patterns can provide the mechanism for both bringing people together and objectively looking at what can be done to alleviate problems.

Types of Conflict. There are a myriad of problems that can emerge as people attempt to work with each other. In general, though, one can often classify conflicts into two broad categories:

- Design/design conflicts. These occur when one person's MAP conflicts with another person's MAP.

- Design/task conflicts. These occur when one is being asked to do work which is opposite his or her MAP.

Let's look at some examples of design/design conflicts.

- You like working within well-understood guidelines and parameters, but your subordinate prefers fluid situations.

- You are motivated to be unique, but your supervisor seeks to meet standards.

- You like to gain mastery, but your co-worker is motivated to make it work.

- You want to be a team member, but you're working with a key contributor, and you see this person as a prima donna.

- You like to coach and encourage, but your co-worker likes to work independently.

- You are motivated to meet all the requirements, but you are teamed up with someone motivated to explore.

Now let us look at some examples of design/task conflicts:

- Being required to give a quick and dirty report when you are motivated to do everything comprehensively.

- Having to spend two months revising an old manual when you are motivated to create from scratch.

- Being put in charge of a program's ongoing maintenance when you are motivated to build.

- Being asked to lay out a detailed plan and follow it when you are motivated to adapt and react spontaneously to situations.

- Having to submit your ideas in writing when you are motivated to interact with people and influence in person.

- Work that requires you to stay on top of detail when you are motivated not to do so.

Adjusting To Conflicts.   Conflicts between people—and between people and tasks—are a natural part of living and working in organizations. As we live and work, we continually move in and out of potential conflict situations and, whenever possible, attempt to shape the situations and people to fit with our perceptions.

Some people are more naturally gifted in adapting to people and situations, some are more naturally gifted in shaping or prevailing. When you can step back and understand the dynamics of how a person's MAP (and your MAP) affects a situation or others, then you are in a better position to determine how best to react or proceed. Many people end up hurting themselves by reacting too strongly to conflicts with others or conflicts with tasks.

No job is perfect and no relationship is perfect. A goal should be to put yourself and your employees into work situations that are reasonably good fits with MAPs. Work is much more rewarding when it engages the Motivational Pattern. However, at times we all find ourselves in work that doesn't engage our MAP or is opposite to it. This is when it gets more difficult. This is when it is best to step back, evaluate, and determine to what extent it is in one's best interest to adjust and compromise.

Understanding, adjusting, and compromising is critical. There are times, though, when the fit is not good at all, and that is when it is best to change situations. Keeping yourself or an employee in a role that is a poor fit will have a detrimental effect on the organization, as well as on you and the person. To be an effective manager it is important to understand this and to make the right decisions.

Enhancing Team Effectiveness

Over the past ten years, one's ability to manage within a team context has become more important. An increasing number of organizations are adopting highly-matrixed structures, building alliances, or forging joint ventures that require effective team skills. Many of us have also seen companies, large and small, flounder because senior management, middle management, a project team, product team, reengineering team or any kind of team, work against themselves.

When People Management consultants assist teams, the problems or blockages encountered within the teams are often MAP conflicts between team members.

"He calls this detailed analysis."
"He never listens."
"Could you follow what she was saying?"
"She's never willing to commit to a schedule."
"Can you believe those calculations?"
"I just don't have confidence in his ability to negotiate this thing."
"It's always got to be his ideas."
"I wouldn't raise that, she's likely to take your head off."

As we have stated previously, we all perceive what needs doing through the eyes or screen of our Motivational Patterns. How we interact, react, feel what needs to be focused on, has merit, should be moved forward, tabled, researched—where the effort needs to go, the larger strategy, the steps to get there are all colored by our perceptions. The following excerpts from an article ("Unique Perspectives on Communication") by Jonathan Moneymaker illustrates this well.

Each of us has a unique world view . . . we each create our own picture of reality.

We create this picture by limiting and editing the information we let in. We must edit; we cannot possibly cope with all the stimuli impinging on our senses. So we selectively attend and selectively perceive, which allows us to superimpose order on what would otherwise be a blur of raw experience. . . . However, we must realize that we are not objective—not neutral—about what we filter and how.

There are several types of filters in operation simultaneously. These filters are responsible for what information gets in. To say that we consciously choose these filters would be an overstatement, but our design is the chief arbiter of which filters we will use. . . .

Some researchers tell us that the human eye can take in about 5 million points of light or bits of information per second, but the revolving power of the brain is approximately 500 bits per second. What does this mean? Selection is inevitable! Can you feel where the chair you're sitting in presses against your back? How does it feel? Now that I've called attention to it, you realize that you have been in contact with your chair all along, but it has not been your primary focus (I hope!). By definition, we cannot "concentrate" on everything. Selective Attention is the filter which decides which cues are important and which are not.

We all selectively attend every day in general ways. Selective Attention is the reason you look at yourself first when you look at a group photo. It's the reason you look at your son or daughter most, out of all the children in the school play. This is Selective Attention on a small scale.

However, we are also saying that your design influences your Selective Attention in more fundamental ways, because the only way a stimulus becomes a stimulus for me is by virtue of what I was already preoccupied with. From all the whole range of available stimuli, I pick out, or selectively attend to, those elements most relevant to my own needs–in other words, relevant to my design.

People are constantly screening available stimuli, and consciously or unconsciously selecting which bits to pay attention to while ignoring others. . . .

We are not passive receptors but active agents in making sense out of sensation. In general, people will notice things that correspond to some element in their design, and will delegate to the background those items of no direct relevance to their own needs and interests. This has profound implications for understanding arguments and conflicts between individuals.

Once we have selected which cues we will allow in, we use selective perception to interpret—or make sense of—these raw cues. All of us, no matter what talent or temperament are continually engaged in making sense out of the world around us. . . .

Our brain separates the wheat from the chaff on the basis of whatever feelings, needs, attitudes and motives are dominant at the moment. The remaining bits of information are relegated to the status of an "unnoticed remainder. . . ."

Communication experts estimate that as we listen to others, most of us are actually only paying attention about 25-50% of the time. We are constantly looping in and out. Sometimes it's because of boredom—meaning that the person is giving us nothing whatsoever that engages any aspect of our design. But just as frequently this looping happens because the person we're listening to has said something that does particularly trigger our interest (meaning specifically that it engages our design in some way), and this starts a parallel train of thought.

Let's imagine that 10 people are listening to a company executive announcing a new procedure. We would hardly suppose that all 10 listeners would be tuning in and out simultaneously. Since each person's selective attention is different, each person will take away different raw data from which he or she will construct a "message." Consequently, this raw data will differ—sometimes considerably—from person to person. Each person's individual design is the major influence in whether they listen for the standards they will be expected to meet, whether the procedures are set in concrete or if they have room to customize, whether the logic behind the proposal is sound, whether the presenter really seems to believe what he or she is saying, or whether they will be able to excel at this new procedure. And, thanks to selective perception, they each bring different needs and predispositions to their interpretation of that raw data. So later, when they get together to discuss "the speech," they are actually discussing "the speech I heard and what I did with it," and are often puzzled by their neighbor's interpretation: "I didn't hear him say that . . ."

. . . we simply do not see the world in the same way. A fundamental reason for defensive behavior is our inability to acknowledge differences—differences between our perceptions and reality, and differences between our perceptions and those of others. The greatest barrier to understanding another person's point of view is your own point of view. . . .

We are never in direct contact with reality. All of our perceptions and conclusions come from filtered information, and our design is the key element in shaping our filters. The world we assemble inside our heads is the only world we know, and each of us is at the center of his or her own world. This is a problematic characteristic of being human. However, we need to realize that "our world" is really a highly filtered experience of those stimuli we choose to allow in. It is this world that we talk about and argue about. Once we acknowledge this disposition, not only in ourselves but in all persons, we are much better able to begin to compensate for it.

Conversely, anyone who naively continues to harbor the notion that he or she is in touch with "the world as it really is" will find life in a team and life in the community continuously threatening, for there are many who share your presupposition, but not your perspective.

When teams are successful, it is because the people involved have blended their unique styles together in such a way that positives far outweigh negatives. Perhaps there is a peacemaker who keeps the group from feeding on itself, or an inspirer who keeps everyone excited. Perhaps the team members share a common approach like always thinking in terms of customer needs or out-of-the-box, creative thinking that binds them together.

When teams start to break down, the root of the dysfunction can usually be traced to conflicts between the Motivational Patterns of people on the team. Whether a team is functioning well or poorly, its performance can be enhanced if each team member understood and appreciated the distinctiveness of each other. The following illustrates this point.

It's All In the Approach

Several years ago I was brought in to assist a team that had worked well together but was beginning to experience some turbulence. The CEO had been through the Motivational Patterning process many years earlier and found the experience insightful and helpful in learning about himself and how to be more effective individually as a leader and manager of his company. There were five key members on his team, one being new (hired about one year ago) and the others, longer-term employees.

As I delved into the concerns, listening to the thoughts of each team member, conducting achievement interviews and developing the MAPs, there were a lot of observations I made. One of the more critical ones revolved around the team's basic approach to addressing issues. The CEO and the longer-term team members had a common approach which involved being very linear and analytical. As a group, they would calmly start at the beginning and work their way through an issue—generally one at a time. Each person brought varying perspectives; i.e., people-focused, bottom-line financial-focused, customer-focused, product-focused, etc.

They settled into a way of interacting where they tended to defer to the expert, listen to what the expert had to say, and then rationally, logically analyze to come up with a solution or plan.

When the team was expanded to a fifth person, the problems started. Everyone recognized that; however, the new executive was liked and all felt he was effective.

His approach was not analytical in a linear way. He tended to move conceptually and intuitively and enjoyed asking probing questions. Although his style added significantly to discussions, it also threw the group off of its linear path. These were subtle detours that went undetected as opposed to major reroutes.

The team recognized that this was causing a problem. They also agreed to be open to feedback from each other. Their solution was to make rational decisions whenever detours arose—should we stay on the path or take the detour. As a result of the insight each person gained about himself or herself and about the other executives, the team enhanced its performance.

Outstanding organizational performance is often directly attributable to the strengths and motivations of the people who are responsible for performance—the management team. A team is at its strongest when it is harnessing each team member's strengths and focusing those strengths on organizational and team needs, without sacrificing the distinctiveness of individual team members. Organizations and the teams that manage them could enhance performance and effectiveness by:

- Identifying issues that it faces, particularly the critical ones.

- Determining the motivated strengths of each team member.

- Having individual and group sessions to enable each team member to understand his or her own, as well as each others, motivated strengths.

- Working at ways to more effectively utilize each other's strengths to meet organizational, team, and individual needs.

It is easy to talk about enhancing team performance, but true team effectiveness means making the commitment to learn about yourself and others and to use that knowledge to work more effectively together. The difficulty many people have in doing this has to do with a lack of comfort in coming to terms with the potentially negative aspects of one's own MAP and little interest in opening that awareness up to others. Without this type of understanding, appreciation, acceptance, and collective awareness and support, a team will be inherently limited. Without the freedom to "deal with" individual MAPs and their impact on each team member, the organization and decisions, then maximum effectiveness can never be obtained.

Improving Job Fit

At People Management, we are often working on issues related to job fit regardless of the application. We are either helping individuals to make good decisions about their work and lives or helping organizations to make good decisions about people. We operate on the simple premise that when an individual's MAP aligns well with the job, then the chances of success and satisfaction improve dramatically.

Making a decision about a person's "fit" to a job is, at times, quite easy, but it can also be very difficult. Clear "yes's" and "no's" exist in many of our consulting sessions as do lots of "maybe's."

In determining "job fit," there are two angles from which to take a view. First is the individual and his or her MAP. Second is the job and what it really entails. The more accurate the picture a person has of the job, the easier it is to make a "job fit" determination.

For example, if people are not motivated to influence others or build relationships, it is clear that they should not be in sales roles. If they are not motivated to analyze, then they should not be in roles dealing with a lot of complexity. If the job involves taking care of details and making sure that everything is done accurately, then hire a person who is so motivated. The key to these statements and the hundreds like them is the surety in knowing what is really needed on the job. To properly determine job fit you must compare your MAP to the details of the job and what it takes to be successful.

Let's look at a few cases of "job fit" to illustrate. The first case is that of a young person, who was in the early stages of his work life, and was trying to make a basic cut decision to get himself into an area where he would have a better chance of thriving.

The Auditor

Several years ago, the head of an accounting firm asked me to assist his son who had recently graduated from college and was now into his sixth month as an auditor with a national accounting firm. Despite the fact that he had received excellent grades in college and was performing well on the job, he was feeling "boxed in" and "unhappy" and not really sure why.

When we did his MAP, his achievements were full of examples where he took ideas or concepts (often his own) and worked to develop them into something tangible. When he was a young child he spent countless hours building elaborate structures with LEGO and Erector sets which he turned into a museum. When he was ten years old, he started a neighborhood newspaper.

In junior high school, the achievement he spoke of involved theatre productions, and he went into detail about conceptualizing the roles he played and shaping himself to play the parts. In high school, he became involved in junior achievement and found the whole process of deciding on a product and marketing it quite rewarding.

In college he wanted to talk about the need to raise money to fix up the fraternity house and the business he put together using students to do odd jobs. During an internship, he was assigned to a product manager and got involved in doing financial calculations for a new product.

When he saw the themes within his own achievements, it was clear to him (and to his father) that he was trying to fit himself into the role of an accountant which was not a good match with his Motivational Pattern. Within a few months, he was able to secure an entry level position within a marketing and product development group, where his first assignment was to participate in upgrading a product line. He was now on a path that fit him better. He now had the type of soil, fertilizer, and climate to better grow and thrive.

In helping this young man to determine if the new position would be a "good fit" or not, I kept him focused on one question: What is needed to be successful on this job? I forced him to look beyond title, money, prestige, and the vague sense of "it feels right." I kept asking: "What do they want you to do? And, "How do they want you to do it?" As he got answers to those questions, he felt more sure that the path was the correct one.

As people move down career paths, decision making as to "job fit" can often become more difficult and subtle. The following illustrates this.

What I Say Is Not What I Mean

I spent hours with this one client, climbing inside his head to understand the job that he had available. There were five candidates to be evaluated for the position, and this needed to be done quickly. "No, I don't think I need to have my own MAP done— I know myself pretty well," he said, "but I would like you to help me decide if any of these five are right for the job."

So I asked a lot of questions about the company and how it works and the "culture" and, in particular, about the job and what he wanted the person to accomplish and how he preferred the new hire to accomplish things. The picture was clear.

The general manager with whom we were working needed a solid operational person to whom he could trust to make sure the work got done—orders filled, staffing appropriate, records kept accurately, realignments made on the floor as needed, people held accountable, etc. "I need to free myself up from the day-to-day," he kept saying, "but I don't have a person I can trust . . . someone who will not check with me all the time. I need to concentrate on client relations and business expansion and not get bogged down with daily operational details."

Several of the candidates were strong fits with the position, and the general manager hired one. Six months later, the hired person (vice president of operations) called me and said, "He's smothering me . . . this isn't going to work . . . he's micromanaging me . . . delegation to him means 'do it my way.' "

In an attempt to salvage the deteriorated relationship between the two, we developed a MAP on the general manager and contrasted it (Compatibility Report) with the head of operations. Despite his words about hiring someone who would operate independently, the general manager really worked best with an operational manager who would carry out his commands.

At first the general manager resisted the nature of his MAP. He kept saying, "That's how I used to be, but I'm not that way anymore." Even though he intellectually knew that he needed to evolve his role and extricate himself from day-to-day operational issues, it was very difficult for him because that was precisely where his motivational interests were.

The general manager was not able to adjust his orientation and control the downside of his MAP. He stayed closely involved in operational detail. As a result, the vice president of operations resigned to accept another job. The general manager did, though, with our guidance hire a person to work with him on business expansion and customer relations. To this person the general manager gave enough freedom. He recognized that the hired person was naturally more interested and gifted in those areas than he was and thus it was easier for him to delegate.

When the fit is clearly "yes" or "no," it is because the contrast between the MAP and the job is obvious. A lot of times the fit is not so clear in that the person has many of the needed aspects but is missing some, or the nature of the Motivational Pattern is both a strength and a potential weakness in the job. In this case, job fit decisions are not easy.

Let's look at another example—one company's attempt to hire a person because the individual's motivated strengths were very needed but where the company also recognized an aspect of the candidate's MAP that was not a good fit.

The Business Developer

The client was a financial services organization, and they hired us to help them select a manager for one of their largest branches. Critical to success in this position was the ability to be visible within the community in order to generate business. One candidate's Motivational Pattern was an outstanding fit for this critical component of the position. However, his MAP revealed little inherent interest in operational areas and making sure that everyday activities were being taken care of.

The client, after much thought, decided to hire the business developer as branch manager and also to bring in a strong operational person as the #2 to ease the operational burden and free the manager to concentrate more on those aspects of the job that fit him best.

The branch manager understood where his motivational interests lay and comfortably worked with and delegated to the #2. The vice president to whom the branch manager reported accepted the limitations and managed to the branch manager's strengths. This arrangement resulted in a significant increase in business within their market.

After two years, the branch manager left to run for political office. He felt that the "fit" as branch manager was "good" but not "great." He was pleased that the organization had recognized his strengths and accommodated them but felt that the administrative and operational details to be taken care of (even though he delegated a lot of them) made the job less satisfying. He found those aspects of work were draining his energy. The parting was very amiable. When the vice president called to tell me that the

           Managing Yourself, Managing Others

branch manager was resigning, he said, "_____ is leaving for precisely the reasons you said that he might."

When you or an employee seeks to evaluate a job opportunity, the MAP can help in making a good decision. Focus in on what is important to you or the employee—what needs to be present to be motivationally hooked. Once armed with that understanding, then look at the job and zero in on what needs doing and how the work needs to be done. Get a picture in your mind as to how someone needs to think and behave in order to be successful in the role, and then match that picture to the MAP and determine where there is "good fit" or "poor fit." By doing this, you will increase your chances of making better decisions. You can also then lay out a plan to minimize the potential downside of those aspects of the job where the "fit" is not good and to maximize the areas of the job where the chances of success are greatest. The following illustrates this.

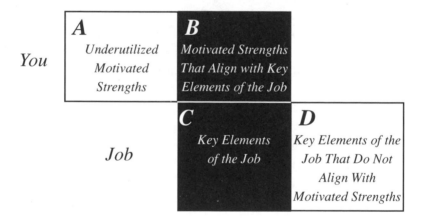

A —   Where motivated strengths are not required by the job. People often find ways to use these outside of paid work.

B&C —   Where motivated strengths fit the job. This is where there is the greatest chance for job satisfaction and success.

D —   Where the job requirements call for motivated strengths that an individual doesn't possess. This is where a person needs to better manage his or her potential weaknesses.

When a job involves the use of employees' motivated strengths, you will find that you need to spend less time overseeing the work of those people. When the job asks that employees work outside of their Motivational Patterns, then you should plan to spend more time overseeing their work.

Improving Job Fit, Work Satisfaction, and Career Decision Making

Most of us live our lives and make decisions about work and careers like contestants on "Let's Make A Deal." We pick a door—not knowing what's on the other side, and hope for the best. Relief after having made the selection is brief—more often than not, new doors and options emerge, and the cycle continues.

Whether you are just beginning your career or are already far along or are seeking to help others—regardless of where you are and what your goal, you can benefit from this section. When people understand their MAPs, they will have a better understanding of what to look for in finding a job or pursuing a career path that fits.

One approach to take in career planning is to be in a position to recognize a good fit job opportunity or career path when it presents itself. This means waiting until something appropriate comes along. A second and more ambitious approach is not to wait for an opportunity to come along but to take actions that could result in landing a job that taps into one's MAP.

As you read through this section, I want you to keep a few things in mind. First, think of a MAP as a picture of one's requirements for work satisfaction. Second, understand that a MAP is an isolated picture of a person in action. Third, a MAP can be well expressed in a number of different jobs. Therefore, people may end up staring at their Motivational Patterns and saying, "Well? So what? How do I make a job decision with it?" Fourth, the MAP becomes most useful as soon as one has something to measure it against. With a MAP as a measuring stick, people should be able to identify work where the fit appears to be strong. For example:

- The person who is motivated to observe detail and has great curiosity, obtains work as a detective.

- A person who is motivated to build and develop obtains a job on the ground floor of a new company.

Or roles that do not fit very well, for example:

- The person motivated to build relationships is transferred to a position where he must lay off a lot of people.

- A person motivated to be sure that all the variables are thought about in advance of a decision accepts the job of doing cold calling.

As you walk through life, you will be faced with dozens of decisions where you will need to assess fit. You will also find that by knowing your MAP, you will be able to more comfortably make decisions that lead to fulfilling results. The key point to remember is that the MAP is most valuable when measured against something specific.

The basic rule to follow in deciding whether one should go into a particular job field is: Don't enter a career with a generalized idea of where it will eventually head. Have a specific idea of the kind of role that best fits as a result of involvement in that field. If research doesn't indicate that a position which fits your MAP will emerge, then another field should be selected.

Let's look at the case of a person who is seeking to pursue a legal career. The question to ask is, "Can that person envision a legal job that will fit his or her Motivational Pattern?"

- Trial lawyer
- Research lawyer
- Rural law practice
- Labor relations

- Politics
- International law
- Corporate lawyer
- Tax specialist

Each of these general areas could be divided and subdivided into many other, more specific job descriptions. Some positions require theatrics, others a love of detail and procedures or; a personal touch with the public or a vast knowledge of previous cases and a desire to research; a desire to exploit potential or serve the public or make a buck for someone.

Going to law school simply because it seems to be where one can earn a lot of money or appears to be "interesting" can lead to a lot of misery. Similarly, going into any job with vague intentions can lead to an unhappy dead end.

In trying to envision the job that could come out of law school or transferring to the marketing area or moving from research to production, consider this—what do you or those that you are advising know about the specifics of that potential job? What does it really require?

The CRs (Critical Requirements) of a job are those attributes, skills, and motivations that are required to successfully perform the task. They are established by the work environment, the boss, the relationships with co-workers, the skills needed to do the job, the subject matter to be worked with, and many other factors.

All of this boils down to research. If people are considering staying in the same field and their potential moves are within their area of personal knowledge, their career decision may simply be a matter of facing the facts revealed in their MAPs and choosing the path which most logically fits them.

This could mean, for example, turning down a promotion. We have found that many people who are not motivated to do certain jobs strive toward them because of the potential to increase one's salary, social pressure, enhanced prestige attached to such positions, or the desire to meet expectations (one's own or others'). This, combined with an inadequate understanding of what the job really requires, can lead people from positions where they are experiencing success and satisfaction to positions where they are dissatisfied, failing or not performing as well as they could.

This type of danger awaits any job seeker, whether entry level or established executive. Failure to comprehend the nature of one's own MAP and the critical requirements of the job can lead to a job mismatch.

Establishing a Job Objective. Knowing what a person is looking for will help that person find or recognize it. Many people who want a different job or something to do with their lives, don't know what it is they are looking for. They only know that they are in pain and they want to get away from that pain. So rather than jump from one bad situation to another, people should first establish what they have to give to an employer. This is often the same thing as what people are motivated to do. By starting this way, people are moving toward something that fits rather than away from something that doesn't fit. One of the best ways to create this job objective is to synthesize the elements of one's MAP into a single statement. There are many ways of pulling those pieces together, but here is one approach that can be used:

1. *A job working with* . . . (Here insert the motivated subject matter: people, ideas, numbers, structural things, and so on.)

2. *Where the conditions of work are* . . . (Here insert the motivated circumstances: project-oriented, require operating under stress, allow some freedom of movement, and so on.)

3. *Where I can operate* . . . (Here insert the preferred way of operating with others: as a member of a team, in a defined role, in a leadership capacity, or other role.)

4. *Using my motivated abilities to* . . . (Here insert the motivated abilities: investigate for the facts, analyze their significance, improvise a solution, organize others, oversee the implementation, and so on.)

5. *Which leads to* . . . (Here insert the central motivational theme: a finished product, chance for advancement, greater responsibility, recognition for my contribution or other central theme.)

In completing this, use whatever filler words to make it flow and help you to communicate the strengths in a clear, easily understood manner. In its "almost finished" form, it should look like the following:

A Sample Job Objective: A job working with people, merchandise, and money—where the conditions of work are not too structured and allow me to tackle and solve problems that come up, and require me to keep a cool head in the face of a lot of pressure; where I can operate pretty much on my own; using my abilities to evaluate people, make friends with them, sell them on myself and my product, keep my merchandise neat and orderly and carefully account for my sales and cost of sales; and which leads to opportunity for participation in the ownership or profits of the business.

What is now needed to complete the job objective (beyond synthesizing the pieces of one's MAP as in the example above) is a reference to one or more specific industries or businesses or activities and ideally, jobs or at least functions. For example, the following could be added to the front of the above job objective. "A job in sales, customer service, or sales training for a retail business selling tangible products." Let's now look at a second illustration that makes such reference as well as synthesizes the elements of the MAP.

Another Sample Job Objective: A job in maintenance or industrial engineering in the machine-tool or equipment-manufacturing industry, working with machinery and its maintenance—where the conditions of work make clear what is expected of me, and each job can be completed before going to the next; where I can operate with others as part of a team; using my abilities to learn how new machinery works, set up a maintenance schedule, repair broken parts, improvise with what is available, and explain to operators how to properly use the machinery; and which leads to opportunity to work with greater variety and complexity of machinery.

Keep in mind that the goal is to start with an ideal job objective, and that it is unlikely that you or anyone that you are assisting will find a position with every element of the MAP being utilized. However, for the basis of comparison, it is good to have a concise statement of what one is shooting for, even if it is idealized somewhat. Taking the time to synthesize the elements of one's MAP in this way gives people a compact, more readily understood way of remembering it—a goal to aim at in career planning and a means of evaluating a particular job fit.

With an ideal job objective in hand, a person will be better prepared to network to identify "good fit" opportunities.

Determining the Critical Requirements of a Job

As discussed previously under Improving Job Fit, getting a clear understanding of what is needed to perform well in a job is critical if the intention is to make good decisions about particular jobs or in career planning.

The first level of determining fit requires minimal analysis, but it can be an effective way of making rough-cut decisions. If the job that is being looked at has relatively simple functions, this could be as far as one needs to go in order to make a decision. While performing "armchair analysis," here are some of the questions or points to consider:

- What abilities are required?
- What will be worked with (subject matter)?
- What are the working circumstances?
- What will be the working relationship with others?
- What is the essential nature of the work?

If the fit looks good, then one can proceed forward a bit more certain that the decision is a good one. If the fit is not good, then the opportunity should be eliminated.

The Critical Requirements (CR) Interview is a process people can use to enable them to get past superficialities and down to the essential requirements of the job by asking questions to determine what the employer wants done and how they want the work done. Ideally, the CR interview should be done with the boss and with the person who is currently in the job or who performed it or a similar job previously. By understanding how the work needs to be done and comparing that awareness to their MAP, people can significantly improve their chances of making good decisions. Let's look at a brief excerpt from a CR interview.

Employer: You'll be supervising a small office.

Candidate: Could you describe the environment here and ideally how you would like this person to supervise the office?

Employer: People here are reluctant to try new things, and we have just invested a lot in upgrading our systems and technology, and so we really need a supervisor who can give people the confidence to step out of their comfort zones.

Candidate: Interesting. What approach would work best in getting people to do that?

As you can see, the basic approach is similar to Achievement Interviewing (described in Appendix A). You're trying to get past generalities and down to the essential requirements. You do this by probing for examples or illustrations of each critical requirement. Begin by asking:

- What is it that you want accomplished in this job?

- What do you see as the real critical requirements of the job, the criteria that will be used to judge performance?

As information is provided, ask "door opening" kinds of questions which will allow you to get at details. For example:

- What is involved in handling the customers?
- How do you go about setting up your day's run?
- Could you give me more details on how you provide market services?
- What are the detailed steps in making such a survey?
- How do you do that?
- What do you mean by coordinate?
- What's involved in that?

You may not have a detailed job description, and as a candidate, one certainly doesn't want to antagonize a prospective boss, but the point here is that the more a person can pin down the details of the job, the easier it will be to determine job fit.

The Decision

As people get good answers to their questions, they should begin to have a clearer idea of whether a job will fulfill most of their requirements. Rarely, if ever, does anyone get a perfect match. In general, people will benefit by establishing criteria as to how far they are willing to go in compromising their MAPs. Comparing what can be uncovered to the following critical job fit questions can be very revealing.

- What elements of the MAP appear to be a strong fit with this job?
- What are the elements of the MAP that this job does not require or allow for?
- If success and satisfaction is achieved in this job, it will probably be because . . .
- If failure or lack of satisfaction results in this job, it will probably be because. . .
- Is there a good fit?

The decision is a personal one. Obviously our recommendation is that a person should compare each part of his or her MAP with each ingredient that is an essential part of the job. Does the job allow one to exercise his or her Motivational Theme? Will the person work with the kinds of Subject Matter found in the pattern? Are the Circumstances present in the job of motivating value? Does the job allow one to Operate with people the way he or she prefers? Will the person be able to use his or her Motivated Abilities?

As people move toward making decisions, only they can say how much of a compromise is acceptable. It would be naive to assume that people will go straight into a job that fits 100%. In fact, it is unrealistic to expect any job to fit 100%. People may want to take a 60% (or less) job fit for the next two years if they know it will lead to a higher paying, 80% job fit down the road. And, of course, people may have other personal considerations that limit or alter their final decision.

The decision is personal, but if people take the time to apply the techniques suggested in this section to all of their career decisions, they will increase their chances of success and, thus, their chances to have a more productive and happier life.

As a manager, you can help your employees to evaluate their career objectives and opportunities that emerge using the techniques outlined here. Many people, in absence of focusing on job fit, focus on title and dollars. And, although important, as the primary or only criteria, it often leads to poor decisions.

Enhancing the Learning Process

I want to touch upon learning and how knowledge of a person's MAP can enhance the learning process. In doing so, I want to broaden your understanding of SIMA by briefly discussing the world of education and selecting an illustration from that world. In doing so, I trust that the words will have relevance to you and those for whom you have responsibility.

Educational institutions are not unlike other organizations that need to be well-managed. If the school is filled with teachers who are not highly motivated to teach, and administrators who are not interested in administration, then success is not likely to be had. Using SIMA to select people who fit the roles for which they are being considered could vastly improve the educational process.

Beyond this is the reality that not all people learn in the same way or for the same reasons. Many children give up on the educational process before they reach adulthood because they don't fit with what is happening in the classroom. A lot of children develop a sense of incompetence or low self-esteem because, try as they may, they have difficulty performing well. So they give up, muddle along, or do not achieve all they could. How many students really maximize their educational experiences?

Imagine a school where an understanding of Motivational Patterns is prevalent throughout and used to help children to better learn their studies and to better learn how to manage strengths and potential weaknesses.

Imagine the teacher or counselor providing support or adjusting the educational approach based upon an understanding of what motivates a child to perform at his or her best. Imagine the acceptance that can be achieved from a parent who might otherwise communicate disappointment.

The Failing Child

I was asked to counsel the son of an executive who had just had his own MAP done. During the feedback session with the executive, he shared with me his tremendous frustration and disappointment with his fourteen-year-old son who was failing in school and drifting toward the darker side of adolescence. What was once a happy, confident child who seemed to like school was now a passive child who seemed to be just putting time in. The child went through the Motivational Patterning process because his parents said he should.

There was one achievement related specifically to education. In fifth grade, he was asked by his teacher to represent his class by participating in a group with other students to discuss topics dealing with growing up in America. He recalled feeling very alive—thinking, talking, and interacting with others. His other achievements similarly involved being part of a group or team where ideas were discussed and a sense of camaraderie prevailed. He liked playing midget football and how each person on the team "worked together." He spoke of learning the plays and performing his role well, but he emphasized that he learned them by talking with others and practicing. He recalled going on vacation once and being involved in a kid's camp at a beach resort where, as a group, they searched for shells and sea creatures and then talked about their discoveries.

What I saw emerge was the MAP of a young person who was motivated to learn by being part of a group that was engaged in active learning and discussion as opposed to doing reading and writing assignments alone. During elementary school he did fine, but when he entered junior high school, the educational experience changed.

He told me that he felt dumb and thought that something was wrong with him because he had a difficult time concentrating, couldn't do well, and felt like he wasn't connected to anything.

He was so preoccupied by this that he just began to withdraw which compounded his negative thoughts even more. When I explained to him how he prefers to learn and assured him that nothing was wrong with him, he seemed relieved and began to loosen up. I explained how Motivational Patterns worked and how this had an impact on him and his mood. He was very engaging during this discussion.

The problem is that most public school systems are not designed to adjust to accommodate individual learning styles. Fortunately the child's family was willing to make an investment in a private school that prided itself on a lot of interactive and team supportive learning. This tapped into the child's motivation and the environment energized him. This positive learning situation, combined with his new awareness of himself, gave him the determination to be disciplined when necessary to do his school work alone.

Enhancing Relationships

I am going to continue to digress a bit more as I focus on improving relationships. I want to use the family setting, because for many of us, the members of our families are the most important people to us. As the organization, Family University, has so appropriately communicated, if one's family and parental situation is out of balance, then one's health and work is likely to suffer. As in the preceding section, I trust that the words will have relevance to you and those for whom you have responsibility.

Several years ago, we received a request from an individual who had previously had his MAP done. This individual had also spent time in sessions with members of his work team sharing each other's MAPs, the goal being to improve understanding and expectations and to make adjustments that would lead to enhanced working relationships.

He called asking me to put his family (spouse and two children) through the process and to help them better understand each other. My first reaction was that I was not a family therapist. I do, though, recognize that SIMA can provide people with a unique perspective that can be beneficial whenever people are interacting with each other.

Family relationships are similar to working relationships in that people interact, and those interactions can have an impact somewhere between uplifting the spirit to destroying it. Much of the impact, positive or negative, is a result of expectations that we place on others. Expectations can motivate:

"He never gave up on me."
"He pushed me beyond what I thought I could do."
"I was determined to prove to him that I could do it."
"Her expectations were high and I didn't want to let her down."

Expectations can also be demotivating, and not meeting them can produce a feeling of failure or poor self-esteem.

"No matter how hard I tried, I couldn't make him happy."
"I did it because she wanted me to, not because I wanted to."
"I could never live up to her image of me."
"His expectations were impossible to achieve."

The Buried Artist

She was in her early seventies when she called. She had read about SIMA because her daughter had left an article during the last visit. She read it and decided to have her MAP done. She didn't want her husband to know. He would not approve. She was restless and beginning to feel unproductive and unmotivated—her energy level was low. She wanted to take courses at the local college, to take up painting, to write a book, to do something but she wasn't sure what. Her husband wanted her to "enjoy retirement" and to take it easy. She lived thousands of miles from our offices so I made an arrangement to provide the services over the telephone.

The Motivational Pattern that emerged was that of an artist who liked to experience and then use that experience to express and create. Most of her life had been spent cooking, cleaning, and raising children. Occasionally she found opportunities to express herself, but almost always within the confines of her defined role. She gave good dinner parties, the house was decorated well, and she helped her children and grandchildren to draw and paint. As a child she talked of singing, dancing, and drawing.

I taped the achievement interview, as I usually do, gave her some instant feedback, followed up with a report (plus sent along the tape), and waited to hear from her in order to set up the feed-back/application counseling session. Before the week was out, I had a call from her husband. I braced myself. He had just finished listening to the tape and reading her MAP report and the supportive material I sent with her MAP. He said, "I've been married to this woman for almost fifty years, and I feel like I never really knew her." He then asked to have his own MAP done.

At last report they restructured roles. He shops, cooks, and takes care of a lot of the everyday business (which he is motivated to do), which freed her up to learn painting and sculpting. She was also planning to get involved with a local theatre group. Her energy level shot up.

Rather than living within the confines of her husband's expectations and, to some extent, the role she grew accustomed to playing and burying the force of her Motivational Pattern, she improved the marriage relationship. To his credit, the husband didn't resist and was able to adjust his expectations which made the changes easier to undertake.

The ability to accept people and not try to force them to be something they are not is critical in relationships. The following story between father and son illustrates this.

Acceptance

A family therapist called and asked that I provide career counseling to the son of an executive and owner of multiple businesses. The nineteen-year-old son was drifting, she said.

When he showed up in our offices, he immediately impressed me with his charm and self-assuredness; but as he opened up, I saw a young man who was exhausted, drained, and demoralized. His mother died when he was nine. His father raised him to be a businessman with the plan for him to work in, and eventually take over, the family business. The son was sent to college and majored in finance and accounting. He failed and returned home. His father was not very forgiving. He wanted his son to be more "determined" and "tough" for that is how you will "make it in this world."

Reluctantly, the father agreed to family counseling because the son was beginning to express his frustration—alternating between violent explosions and a "whatever you say" attitude.

The Motivational Pattern of the son revealed a gentle spirit who wanted to meet the needs of others—the type of person who wanted to listen to others and nurture, take care of, and help them. In his fantasies, he dreamed of joining the Peace Corps, helping the underprivileged, assisting in a nursing home. He resisted these thoughts as much as he could and tried to shape himself to be a hard-nosed businessman. He tried to meet his father's needs and expectations and almost destroyed himself and the relationship in the process.

I never met the father. At first he wanted nothing to do with me or People Management. More than one year later, I received a Christmas card from the father thanking me. Although the family counselor didn't tell me what had transpired, I suspect that she had the motivational drive and persistence to arm wrestle the father to submission—to get him to accept and appreciate his son.

Each of us is crafted differently, and the talents and gifts we have all been given are part of the wondrous diversity of this world. Just as you would not expect an apple tree to produce lemons or a camel to run like a cheetah, one should not expect others to be who they are not meant to be. When you allow yourself and your employees to grow and develop within the nature of the motivational design, then you have a greater chance to personally experience, and help others to experience, the fullness of life that we are all meant to experience. And the bottom line is, as a result, we also have the chance to maximize our productivity and to achieve success.

Where Do You Go From Here?

What to do once you have an awareness of your MAP: Rather than develop insights on your MAP and then put the information away in the bottom of a drawer, keep it available and review it periodically to enhance your understanding of yourself. Use it as a base to review times that are good and also times that are frustrating. This way your MAP becomes a living document—one that expands and grows as you expand and grow. Use it to enhance your understanding of your motivated behavior and its implications in all aspects of your life. Use it as a MAP to help you find a path to greater success and productivity.

What to do if you don't have an awareness of your MAP: Either draw your own using Appendix A as a guide, or contact People Management to make arrangements to have one done. You can also become a student of your own behavior—paying attention to when you feel highly motivated. Then use that insight as if you had an awareness of your MAP.

As a manager of people, where do I begin? As a manager, whether you have awareness of your own MAP or not, you can start to use SIMA right away by recognizing that each of the people for whom you have responsibility is motivated differently. If you understand what motivates them to perform their best, then you will be on the road to becoming a more effective manager of people. Start by just watching and listening for the consistency within people. Watch and see when your employees get passionate about work and then try to feed that passion—their Motivational Patterns.

CHAPTER VI

Appreciating the Design of Your MAP

You need not fear that you have no Motivational Pattern. Having a Pattern seems to be an absolute ingredient of being human.

–Arthur F. Miller Jr.

In the book, *Job Shift: How to Prosper in a Workplace Without Jobs*, William Bridges writes of how "societies" have used the "picture of the individual's life as a journey" and "in the image, life events are stepping-stones or crossroads." He speaks of two journeys. The first being an "external" one and the second, a "journey toward becoming the person that you really are." He then tells the story of the "Jewish wise man, Rabbi Zusya," who said shortly before he died, "In the world to come, I shall not be asked, Why were you not Moses? I shall be asked, Why were you not Zusya?"

Bridges then proceeds to emphasize that "In this second journey, we are trying to become the people we are meant to be"—that "we fail to see that most of what the 'great people' of the world have accomplished was not done because they were different but because they were not busy trying to be somebody else."

Bridges sees the world of work changing and jobs, as we know them, he feels are going away. His book is about how to be successful in the new world of work, where people move from employer to employer applying their knowledge and skill; as opposed to remaining with one company. He sees a paradigm shift as change accelerates and the need to be flexible increases. Just as Alvin Toffler (*Future Shock*) emphasized the importance of being anchored in knowing who you are, so does Bridges.

I have seen a lot of sadness in the lives of people as they pursued paths that were not in harmony with the nature of their MAPs. And I have seen the joy when people have emerged from darkness to see a path that "fits."

What is true of individuals is often true of organizations as well. When a company is focused and in harmony with its nature, and when its employees are in roles that fit, then greater productivity is achieved as potential is unleashed. This may sound obvious, but it appears allusive to many organizations and the people who lead and manage them. When it comes down to it, most employers expect their employees to become what they want them to and perhaps this is at the root of poor performance or an inability to maximize the potential within.

Bridges writes of the need to shift from "compliance-based organizations to commitment-based" ones.

> Our need to be more productive is forcing us to reconsider what really motivates a person to do his or her best. . . . Most successful organizations are made up of people doing what they like to do and believe in doing.

Phil Jackson, in his book, *Sacred Hoops*, draws upon ancient teachings to explain how the Chicago Bulls built success. He refers to a Harvard Business Review article that recounts a Chinese fable about the Master, Chen Cen, who said of the first ruler to consolidate China (Liu Bang):

> So it is with a master craftsman like Liu Bang. After placing individuals in positions that fully realize their potential, he secures harmony among them by giving them all credit for their distinctive achievements.

This is a lesson that all leaders and managers should understand and practice. When a person is in an activity that fits, there is harmony. And when there is "fit" and harmony, there is usually success and satisfaction. We have all felt this at some point, and it feels good and right.

When you know the ingredients of who you are and what puts you in a harmonious relationship to the world—and to work, then it becomes a lot easier to achieve that harmony. This is the value in understanding your MAP.

When you experience the joy in doing work that you love, and it reinforces the essence of who you are, it is easier to feel in harmony with the universe and with the uniqueness that resides within.

So Where is All This Going—A Personal Statement

I believe in the goodness of people. I believe that in their hearts and souls, when people start out, that life is an open road, and much can be accomplished if they follow their paths to success. I believe that people:

- Want to be productive.
- Want to be successful.
- Want their lives to be fulfilling.
- Seek purpose and meaning.

I believe that these fundamental drives can be distorted, damaged, and bruised—and can all but disappear—but can never be extinguished, no matter how oppressive life becomes. I believe that if you gain an understanding of your MAP and seek to use it in your work, relationships, and decision making, then you have a tool that you can continually draw upon.

However, as I look at words like success, meaning, and fulfillment, I am humbled by the enormity of those words. These are not words to be dealt with lightly. These are words that get at the core of our being. These are the kinds of words we wrestle with when we are out of sorts, in pain, spinning around, standing not sure where to go, late at night when all the daily distractions are asleep—these are words that say, "Why am I here?" Is it to have fun? as so many of us thought in our youth, or to accumulate wealth or power? which, as some of you have come to know, is a powerful intoxicant. Is it to move up the corporate ladder or just go along or to have children and keep life going? Is it to grow, experience, move forward?

So, before closure is brought, I would like to explore and share some personal thoughts on the subjects of success and finding meaning in your life.

I have been interviewing people on their achievements for over twenty-five years. I see Motivational Patterns unique to each person emerge and stay constant. I believe that genetically we are all predisposed to behave in certain ways unique to our own make up; that we appear to be designed with a pattern of giftedness; that each person seems to have a purposiveness about him or herself—a destiny to his or her life if he or she chooses to allow it to unfold.

I cannot help, sitting in the seat that I do, listening to what I hear and seeing what I do, and not ask a basic question, "If we are designed, then who designed us?" This is no small question, and its exploration has led me down a path I would not have anticipated, given where I started.

I have found in my life that success, meaning, and fulfillment came as my MAP linked up with my belief in God. I have found that when I allowed God to draw me into his embrace, and as I understood and accepted that I have been gifted and that my gifts are to be used to their fullest, then I gained an understanding of the purpose of my life. Your Motivational Pattern, like life itself, is a gift to be used and appreciated.

I have seen in my consulting how people, in their "success," forget that they have been given gifts and are successful only because they have developed the gifts they have been given. I have seen people elevate themselves beyond what is spiritually healthy. I have also seen people bury their gifts and give up on life. Both sadden me. In one is the lost potential and untapped beauty, and in the other, a weakened soul.

I strongly believe that being humbled by your giftedness while at the same time developing it to its fullest, are cornerstones upon which to build a sense of purpose and meaning into your life as well as a way to measure success.

When I saw my own design as part of a larger universe, a sense of meaning came more easily. As my faith grew, so did my understanding of myself and my ability to accept who I am. As I accepted, I grew stronger and more confident in taking risks and letting my Motivational Pattern and life develop. I saw that when you have faith, there is often comfort in knowing that you are not alone and that you are connected to something larger than yourself.

I have come to believe that success, meaning, fulfillment and a sense of purpose come when your destiny is part of a larger design and universe; that when you have faith, you can see the connection more clearly.

Peace . . . comes within the souls of men when they realize their relationship, their oneness with the universe, and all its powers, and when they realize that at the center of the universe dwells the great spirit, and that this center is really everywhere—it is within each of us.

– Black Elk

This all returns me to the word "success." Simply put, success cannot be measured by money, title, or power, although some people try to measure it that way. It cannot be measured by any external standard. People build buildings, pass laws, write books, make sales, earn straight A's, raise good children, represent causes, uphold the law, teach, counsel, manage, lead, and do all kinds of activities and have all types of "successes." But these things do not necessarily make someone's life successful. This is how others look at you and determine success. This is why many people who look to be extraordinarily successful do not feel that they are.

I have observed through my counsel that measuring success can become quite complicated. When all is said and done, your success can only be determined by you.

In the privacy of self-evaluation, I have seen people as they strip away all the external measures of success, or lack of them, and look at what they have accomplished within the larger context. I have seen people wrestle with their lives—at times while they are in the midst of running hard and at times when they are near the end and looking back.

It is at these moments when one is searching, unguarded and receptive to his or her own heart, that a realization often unfolds. When people recognize and accept that they have purpose built in and use their gifts to their fullest to benefit not only themselves but others, then they often feel more successful, and a sense of oneness with their environment; and, when they do not, then they are often left feeling unfulfilled—somehow they could have and perhaps should have done something more.

There are two pieces to this. The first is not dissimilar to what athletes often refer to as being in a "zone." When you are in a "zone," success seems to build upon itself, and you feel a sense of congruence and fit. This is what it is like when you are engaged in activity that fully engages your MAP. Your senses are keen. You're operating at full gear. You're enjoying yourself. You're being successful and can't believe that life can be so good.

The second piece is where you apply your gifts and how self-focused, self-absorbed, and self-serving you are with them. There is nothing wrong with taking care of yourself and extracting the most that you can. But if this is where you remain, then there is no connection to the larger universe that connects us all. If the gifts that you have been given are not used with appropriate stewardship, then meaning and fulfillment will likely elude you.

> To one servant the Master gave five talents; to another, two; to a third, one—each according to his ability. Then he set out—the man who received five, made more—the man who received two, made more—but the man who received one, dug a hole and hid it. When the Master returned after a long absence, He said to the first, "Well done, I will give you more"—to the second He said, "Well done, I will give you more"—the third said to the Master, "I was afraid and went off and hid the talent you gave me." To the third the Master said, "Throw him into the dark."

> From Matthew 25: Parable of the Talents

There are many paths and opportunities that lay before you, and the more you can direct your life and put yourself into positions that allow you to fully use your Motivational Pattern, the more successful and satisfied you are likely to feel and be. The more you can, as a manager of people, assist others and your organization in doing so, the more effective you will be in fostering success. If you can do this, the more meaningful your life will be.

You cannot lose your talent:
but you can fail to use it.
And if you fail in this way, failure in life is the result.

–Benjamin Franklin

Afterword

I grew up not being very good at most things, but I was good in sports and in playing poker and not much else. I used to take the train into New York City and go to 42nd Street and watch people. I liked it when we had a lot of relatives come over for dinner and I could watch the interaction at the dinner table. I was never part of any one group in high school or college because I liked associating with, and observing, all kinds of people. I was good in poker because I could read people and sense the flow of the game—the same in basketball. I got a lot out of my 5' 7" height. I liked listening to people and understanding them—I liked helping people. I loved listening to my father tell stories about his life. My mind always filled itself with observations on what I saw and heard. I remember as a kid reading a psychology book called *The Fifty Minute Hour* from cover to cover at one sitting, absolutely absorbed. I became a student counselor in college because people seemed to like to tell me things, and I liked listening to what they had to say—and then sharing my thoughts and observations. I was never quite sure what I would do with my life. I was like many others who flounder as they struggle to find their place in this world and their path to success. When I was introduced to SIMA in 1975, I instinctively moved towards it. Quite honestly, the whole process came so natural to me that I didn't even think about it at first. I'm still not very good at many things, but I was fortunate enough to stumble into a profession and company where my Motivational Pattern could flourish.

Appendix: A

Drawing Your MAP

*There is no wretched and coarse a soul wherein
some particular faculty is not seen to shine.*

–Montaigne

On the following pages you will find the longer version of the SIMA Biographical Form that we at People Management ask individuals to complete before we conduct the achievement interview. There are three sections to this form. In the first, one is asked to make a list of achievements that range over his or her lifetime. In the second, the person selects achievements from the list that are most important to him or her. In the third, the individual elaborates in writing on those selected. The shorter version merely asks the participant to complete steps one and two.

On the pages that follow the form, you will find rules on how to conduct Achievement Interviewing℠ and techniques on how to convert the data obtained from the form and the interview into a MAP.

THE
SIMA®
BIOGRAPHICAL
FORM

PEOPLE MANAGEMENT
ONE DARLING DRIVE
AVON PARK SOUTH
AVON, CT 06001
(860) 678-8900

System for Identifying Motivated Abilities

Before You Start

If you are like most people, you have never taken time to sort out the things you are good at and motivated to accomplish. As a result, it is unlikely that you use these talents as completely or effectively as you could.

Identification of your strengths and vocationally significant motivations is the purpose of SIMA®.

To complete this form, you are asked to list and describe things you have done that you: 1) enjoyed doing and 2) believed you did well. Such achievement activities may have occurred in your work or your home life or your leisure time.

It is imperative that you put down what was important to you. Do not include an item only because others felt it was important. The activities you list may be quite simple and not impressive to others. They may have nothing to do with success, great accomplishments, fame or fortune. Concentrate on activities that gave YOU a sense of satisfaction. They may have made you feel proud. They may have been just plain fun to do. They may have been a combination of pleasure and pain, but they left you feeling fulfilled, accomplished, proud or otherwise satisfied.

Also, it is essential that you relate specific achievement activities and not general ones. To help you understand the type of achievement activities we are after, you will find below examples of things other people have listed as personally significant.

You will have the opportunity to develop a similar list on pages 140-145.

Summary Examples

"Putting on plays for neighborhood children with costumes, props, etc. The most successful project was transforming a shed in back of our house into a fairyland with lighting effects, decorations, princesses."

"I built and mastered the tallest pair of stilts in my neighborhood. I started a stilt craze among my friends."

"I had a job as a printer's devil. I developed a method of cutting stereotypes which was faster and more accurate than that previously used."

"I established an evening routine of a quiet time of sharing and reading with our children which made bedtime an enjoyable end to the day."

"Was a prime mover in starting a company. Saw utility of product concept. Had much to do with early market development. Helped conceive basic manufacturing concepts."

"Organized and ran a company-sponsored national conference with about 100 participants. Conference was a resounding success."

"Won the support of my subordinates over a period of years by building strong relationships. Took an interest in developing careers, always sent cards on birthdays, Christmas and special events."

It is easy to misunderstand these examples. If you review them again, you will discover that they are:

- Achievement activities, not experiences

- Specific achievements, not milestone achievements

- Activities you can support with examples

By way of explanation, we will contrast good examples with poor ones:

Achievement Activities, Not Experiences

Not: "I toured Europe with my wife and the Alps were beautiful."
But: "I fixed a grandfather's clock when I was 12 years old that hadn't worked for 2 years."

Specific Activities, Not Milestone Achievements

Not: "Got my Ph.D." -or- "Had a baby" -or- "Became Operations Manager."
But: "Made original discoveries in science labs" -or- "Coached my wife during child birth" -or- "Worked with subordinates to improve their skills; improved output by 25%."

Activities You Can Support with Examples

Not: "I'm good at troubleshooting."
But: "Caught a design problem during prototype testing and saved the company over $10,000."

Before you begin to write, read the following principles and tips carefully.

Tips for Completing this Form

- Take enough time to complete the form. On average, it takes between 2 and 6 hours.

- Don't worry about whether or not you can recall impressive childhood achievements. Select any activity you can remember enjoying and doing well. Don't reject it because it seems silly, trivial, or unimportant.

- Write what was important to you, not what was important to your family or to your friends. If some honor or recognition left you cold, leave it out.

- Don't be limited to narrow time frames. If you have enjoyed achievement activities that have occurred over a stretch of years, list them in the long-term (LT) section. If you're proud of them and enjoyed the activity, it's worth documenting.

- When you recall something you did and believe you did well, write it down. Don't try to analyze or evaluate it. We're looking for your history, not your evaluation.

- Don't be modest. You are the key actor in every event. These are your achievements.

The Three Steps

There are three steps in completing this form. The better you complete each one, the more you will enhance our ability to provide you with an accurate description of your Motivated Abilities:

Step 1
Write a summary of your achievement activities. In other words, a list of brief descriptions.

Step 2
Select five of the most important activities from the summary list.

Step 3
Write one-page expansions on each of the selected five.

Remember, there is no time limit to complete the form. IT IS NOT A TEST, so enjoy yourself. There are no right or wrong answers.

PLEASE PRINT (If you are more comfortable using a word processor, feel free to do so.)

Step One

Summary of Achievement Activities

For each period, briefly describe two or more specific things you accomplished that you enjoyed doing and believed you did well. If it would be helpful, put the calendar years covered under the age period; i.e., "59 - 63" – create additional categories for more achievements if you wish to add (a-3, b-3, etc.). If you wish to note long-term achievements, place them under the LT designation at the end of this section. **Please print.**

Childhood
(a-1)

(a-2)

Teen Years
(b-1)

(b-2)

Age _____
(c-1)

(c-2)

Age _____
(d-l)

(d-2)

Age _____
(e-l)

(e-2)

Age _____
(f-1)

(f-2)

Age _____
(g-1)

(g-2)

Age _____
(h-1)

(h-2)

Long-Term Achievement Activities
(LT-1)

(LT-2)

(LT-3)

Step Two

Selecting

Of the things you have described, note in the boxes below the five that are particularly important to you (e.g., b-2, f-1), not necessarily in order of importance. Please place an asterisk(*) next to the summary achievement activities (in Step 1) you have chosen. If possible, try to pick examples from your whole life, not just recent activities.

☐ ☐ ☐ ☐ ☐

Step Three

Expanding On the Most Important Achievement Activities

Taking the five most important activities in the order given in the preceding boxes, describe:

1. How you got involved in it;

2. The details of what you actually did (elaborate and expand); and,

3. What was particularly enjoyable or satisfying to you.

Some individuals like to write, so they will thoroughly enjoy this exercise. Others are reluctant to do this much writing. If you are in the latter category, you might dictate your expansion into a tape recorder and have someone transcribe your words onto the following pages. Likewise, if you are more comfortable using a word processor, feel free to do so.

Try to fill each page, focusing on the details of what you actually did.

Start each page by repeating the summary statement about the achievement.

Achievement Activity (   )   1

One line summary statement:

How you got involved:

Details of what you did (how you actually went about doing it):

What was particularly satisfying to you:

Achievement Activity (   )   2

One line summary statement:

How you got involved:

Details of what you did (how you actually went about doing it):

What was particularly satisfying to you:

Achievement Activity ( ) 3

One line summary statement:

How you got involved:

Details of what you did (how you actually went about doing it):

What was particularly satisfying to you:

Achievement Activity (   )   4

One line summary statement:

How you got involved:

Details of what you did (how you actually went about doing it):

What was particularly satisfying to you:

Achievement Activity (   )   5

One line summary statement:

How you got involved:

Details of what you did (how you actually went about doing it):

What was particularly satisfying to you:

Now that you have completed the SIMA Biographical Form, you are ready to proceed. This involves using your achievements to gain an understanding of your Motivational Pattern.

The next step can be done alone or with others. Taking each achievement, talk about them one at a time. Your goal here is to describe in detail what it is that you did and how you did it. You can interview yourself, which admittedly is quite difficult. You can find a good listener and ask that person to interview you. You can also form a small group of three or four people and have them interview you. Regardless of what you choose, tape record the interview so that what you describe can be examined and used to develop your MAP.

What's critical is that the achievement interview be conducted using certain rules. If the rules are violated, then the data that emerges will not be accurate.

As the interviewer, you never ever ask a leading question or suggest to the person that he or she talk about anything that they haven't already raised themselves. This is much more difficult than it sounds. It requires enormous discipline and concentration.

The following briefly outlines the rules and procedures for Achievement Interviewing. It is through this interviewing process that you will obtain the data that you will need to unveil your MAP.

Achievement Interviewing Rules

The achievement interview is a guided monologue with the person being interviewed talking most of the time. The purpose of the interview is to get as much detail as is practically possible about what the person did in his or her achievements and how he or she did them. This is done by:

- Asking for fact and not opinion.
- Avoiding a tendency to ask leading questions.
- Keeping the person focused on "how" and not "why."

The interviewer starts by reading the achievement as the individual has written it and then asking, "What's the achievement? What did you do that you enjoyed doing and felt you did well?"

After the person being interviewed answers that question, the interviewer asks for an expansion. This means letting the person tell his or her story and looking for opportunities to help the person to amplify what was done and how it was done. The interviewer is always working from what the person writes and says, not his or her own interests. For example:

"You say coordinate. Spell that out if you would."
"Organize? What do you mean? Give me an example."
"What would be an example of somebody you helped?"
"Give me an illustration of some of those problems."
"Give me more details on what you did."
"What was your involvement?"
"Give me some specifics?"

As the interviewer, always work from what people being interviewed say—their words and their phrases. Never explore your own curiosity. When you feel it is time to move onto another achievement, ask the person being interviewed one last question: "What was enjoyable and satisfying about this achievement?" See if anything new occurs to explore.

Remember—

- Avoid areas of interest to you (as the interviewer), and focus on what the person being interviewed actually did.

- Never ask "why"; always ask "how."

One important key to unlocking doors when conducting achievement interviews is to listen for action words and ask the person being interviewed to expand. Action words are always verbs. (I organized, planned, sold, built, etc.) If you stick with the word "how" (how did you organize, plan, sell, build, etc.?), it will be difficult to mess up.

As the person being interviewed, put yourself into the situation and reexperience the achievement. As you do, describe what it is that you are seeing and doing and what is going on in your mind. Don't hold back. Don't worry about how clear you are or how you sound to whoever might be listening. You have inside of you what you need to know, and your job at this stage is to get it all out. Later you will assemble the data into a MAP, but for now, you want to get it all out, onto the tape so that you can use it to guide you on your life journey.

Once you have described in detail your achievements, you will have a gold mine of information on the tape from which you can work. If you have access to a good typist, you are encouraged to transcribe the tape and consolidate the transcript with what you wrote. This is the data you will use to learn about and sketch your MAP.

Drawing Your Map

At People Management, once we have interviewed a person on his or her achievements, we usually take the tape of the interview and have it transcribed. We then pour through the details of the transcript and write a report that describes the themes that we see. The consultants who write the MAP reports go through extensive training to hone their skills, develop their knowledge, and obtain the type of expertise needed.

In some cases, the consultant will spend as much as ten hours to produce a report totaling twenty or more pages. In other cases, the report is short, perhaps only a few pages. Regardless of the report length, the words describing the phenomena that is seen are carefully selected.

Some of you reading this book have already had your MAPs done by People Management or through a PMI sponsored workshop, affiliate or associate, but some of you will attempt to draw your own MAPs.

Clearly your MAP-making skills are not going to be as good as the experts at People Management—this type of expertise can only be developed over time. Recognizing that imperfections will occur and the detail may not be as good, you can still derive great benefit by drawing your own MAP or attempting to do so—even though it might only be a rough sketch.

With this in mind, I am going to suggest several ways that you can proceed to pull the data from your own interview into a MAP, which we'll call an approximated Motivated Abilities Pattern. Even though the process will not yield the type of MAP report we at People Management produce, it should be revealing and useful in helping you to find your path to success.

Whether you are an employee of People Management or someone

who is about to delve into his or her own achievement data, certain rules need to be followed. If the rules are not followed, then the conclusions drawn are not likely to be accurate. These rules are really quite simple.

- Deal with fact, not interpretation or extrapolation. Do this by clustering words and phrases that have similar meaning. Use the clustering process to determine what Circumstances, Abilities, and Subject Matter you are motivated by and what types of Operating Relationship(s) to others you prefer.

- In order for a cluster to be motivated, it needs to appear throughout your achievements, not just once or twice. It doesn't, though, need to appear in all of them.

- The Central Theme must be present in every single achievement. If it isn't, then it is just an element of your MAP. We often create clusters to describe the Central Themes we see. These Themes tend to be more conceptual and the process to determine them usually involves a lot of synthesis.

As the PMI consultants we train to write MAP reports make observations as to motivated themes and elements within a person's MAP, their trainer will continually ask them to point to the evidence to back up their conclusions. If enough evidence cannot be found within the achievement data, then the observation doesn't become part of the MAP. This should be the acid test for all that you select to be part of your MAP—there must be significant evidence from the data to support the observation.

In developing your approximated MAP, our recommendation is that you work from a transcript that has combined the written portion of your SIMA Biographical Form with the spoken words from your achievement interview. This will provide you with the most accurate material with which to work. If you cannot transcribe the achievement interview, then listen to the tape of your interview several times in order to become very familiar with its content. You can also take notes as you listen, writing down words and phrases. As you do so, you want to pay particular attention to:

Action words (verbs)   —   e.g., designed, persuaded, analyzed

Subject Matter (nouns) — e.g., goals, systems, relationships

Significant Comments   — e.g., seeing the result, making a key contri-
                              bution, being one of the guys

Perhaps the easiest approach to producing an approximated MAP is to use a list of words and select those words that most closely represent you. The disadvantage of this approach is that it limits you to the words on the list. What follows is one format used in a PMI sanctioned workshop where participants develop their approximated MAPs.

As you delve into your transcript, your notes, or your recollection from listening to the tape of your interview, respond to each of the questions in this section.

The Checklist Approach

Motivating Subject Matter

Which of the following best describes the types of Subject Matter that you worked on, with, or through in your achievements? Circle no more than two.

- Data, i.e., number, details, words, money, information
- Things, i.e., structures, tools, machinery, materials, plants, phenomena
- Senses, i.e., sound, light, color, texture, taste, movement, manual
- People, i.e., individuals, groups, human behavior, cultures
- Ideas, i.e., concepts, theories, principles, values, thoughts

Motivating Circumstances

Which of the following best describes the types of Circumstances that you worked with in your achievements? Circle no more than two.

- Visibility, i.e., being seen or noticed, in front of others, reputation
- Different, i.e., new, novel, unique, unknown
- Structure, i.e., clear requirements, models, order, clear definition

- Measured, i.e., measurable results, standards, finished product, goals
- Difficult, i.e., pressure, challenges, demand, risks, obstacles, competition

Motivated Abilities

Which of the following best describes how you went about learning the information you needed in your achievements? Circle no more than two.

I Learn By:

- Reading—studying and researching; going through books and other printed materials, maybe taking notes or outlining
- Observing—taking a careful firsthand look; examining the actual detail of a phenomenon, an object or action
- Trying—testing myself while doing the thing I want to learn, trying my hand at particular skills, experimenting to develop my own techniques
- Memorizing—going over and over the thing I want to learn, repeating it until I have it down pat
- Asking—probing, inquiring, interviewing, getting information from people, finding out things by asking people questions
- Conferring/Discussing—getting information through expressing my own thoughts and hearing the thoughts of others in conversation, engaging in give-and-take interaction where information flows both ways—hearing and speaking style of communication

Which of the following best describes how you evaluated the information? Circle no more than two.

I Evaluate By:
- Analyzing—breaking things down or dissecting them into their component parts
- Empathizing—reading people or sounding them out, sensing or

checking out what they are thinking or feeling
- Weighing Pros & Cons—judging merits, choosing or deciding by weighing plus and minuses in the face of risks and uncertainties
- Calculating—choosing or deciding by the "number"—by going over the figures
- Comparing—comparing what I'm observing to established standards or benchmarks
- Assessing Worth—judging the fitness, the advantage or suitability of a resource, thing, or person for a particular use or application

Which of the following best describes how you used the information in order to prepare to take action? Circle no more than two.

I Prepare By:
- Organizing—fitting information, things, people, or ideas together into a well-ordered or systematic whole
- Practicing—getting ready by rehearsing or conducting "dry runs" to make sure I'm ready for a specific upcoming event
- Picturing—using my "mind's eye" to visualize a picture of things (objects, events, or processes) as they're going to be
- Setting Goals—marking out (whether in my mind or on paper) something to shoot for, then focusing my energy and capabilities on getting there
- Strategizing—setting the objective and charting a course that avoids anticipated pitfalls and takes advantage of potential angles and opportunities

Which of the following best describes how you went about getting the job done, or how you took action? Circle no more than two.

I Take Action By:
- Nurturing—fostering growth or development in people or things—nurturing potential
- Creating/Innovating—coming up with concepts, designs, devices, methods, or systems that are new, different, or improved
- Developing—adapting, modifying, blending, synthesizing, expanding, extending, or adding to what already exists

- Physically Doing—getting my body into it, hands-on, physically exerted
- Producing: building, constructing, turning materials into a completed structure or product; making or forming things from raw materials
- Maintaining—repairing, replacing, cleaning; keeping the machine or the operations oiled, polished, and running effectively
- Operating—getting the task done by driving; handling the controls; running the machines, the vehicles, or equipment
- Overseeing—getting things done through monitoring, coordinating, facilitating, or directing the actions of others; or by managing their talents

Which of the following best describes how you caused others to take action or informed them about what you did or knew? Circle no more than two.

I Influence By:
- Bargaining—striking a deal, whether in confrontational "horse trading" or in collaborative "wheeling and dealing"
- Getting Others Involved—mustering the troops, building up participation, involving people—in activities, programs or causes
- Motivating—stirring others into action by firing them up with ideas or by appealing to needs or emotions; inspiring others, or renewing their confidence
- Conversing—expressing my own thoughts in a discussion
- Counseling—drawing on my experience and expertise to help people solve problems and make decisions
- Teaching—stirring interest, challenging or encouraging others to inquire; preparing people to perform certain tasks or responsibilities; providing examples, demonstrations and illustrations
- Writing—presenting ideas, information, or narrative using the written word; using just the right word to clarify a point or to present the full dimensions of a thought
- Suggesting—putting ideas on the table, and initiating actions; starting the ball rolling by taking the first step or by tossing out an idea
- Persuading—convincing, advocating, winning people over to my

point of view by the force of a convincing argument
- Performing—making an impact or impression by acting out a part, presenting an idea, demonstrating a skill or talent

Motivating Relationships

Which of the following best describes the type of Relationship you revealed in your achievements? Circle only one.

- Individual Contributor—want to get results primarily through my own efforts and bring them to others
- Influencer—want to have an effect on others and/or influence them to take action, but do not want responsibility for their overall management
- Overseer—want to take responsibility for results other people produce by directing, leading, coordinating, or managing their performance

Which of the following best describes how you related to authority in your achievements? Circle only one of the following.

- Hands Off—"Let me do my own thing."
  I function most effectively under an authority who allows me to exercise independent control over my specific area of responsibility.
- Collaborative—"Let me work with you."
  I function most effectively under an authority who treats me as an equal, who works with me as though I were involved in a joint effort, and who has a genuine interest in my ideas and suggestions.
- Supportive—"Give me help when I need it."
  I function best under an authority who provides me with direction and support at key points of my involvement in a task.

Central Motivational Thrust or Theme

Which of the following best captures the underlying Theme in your achievements? Circle only one.

- Personal Performance—comparing and contrasting my achievements with the way others perform or against customary standards
- Impact or Effect—improving results, improving the performance, getting a response, extracting potential, fixing things, shaping, leaving my mark
- Personal Power—owning results, overcoming obstacles, exercising power over people and things, developing mastery-level skill, understanding the whole thing
- Achieving a Goal—reaching a target, completing the job, satisfying the needs, passing the test, fulfilling the requirements, making the grade, or meeting expectations
- Engaging In A Process—pioneering, discovering the new, building proficiency, advancing a technology, making ideas a reality, developing a product or process

Once you have gone through the checklist and determined which words most closely represent you, then summarize your conclusions using the MAP outline that follows. You now have in a concise format a valid image of your Motivational Pattern. Rather than leave it hidden in a book, copy it onto a piece of paper and keep it in a place where you can periodically review it or use it to make better decisions.

Map Outline

Central Theme   _____

Motivating Subject Matter   _____

Motivating Circumstances   _____

Motivating Abilities   _____

    Learn by   _____

                  _____

    Evaluate by   _____

                  _____

    Prepare by   _____

                  _____

    Take Action by   _____

                  _____

    Influence by   _____

                  _____

Motivating Relationship   _____

Preferred Relationship to Authority   _____

The Unstructured Approach

Whereas some of you will find comfort in the boundaries of guide sheets and checklists, others will find their use restrictive. This second method approaches the MAP development process in a free-flowing manner. In this approach, you write down the observations you can make—the themes for which you can see evidence. You don't become concerned about format.

This method may not produce a formal-looking report, set up according to the five ingredients of a MAP, but it should produce significant insights as to your motivated behavior. Once you have those insights, then you can use them to make more effective decisions about life and work. You can also use those insights as a jumping-off point to become a better student of yourself.

In recommending this approach, I recognize that some of you will be motivated to carry it out and will do so with minimal encouragement, and for others, this will be a real chore. This is, after all, the nature of the Motivated Pattern.

Combination Approach

For those of you who prefer to have a bit of structure (as in the checklist approach) and freedom to synthesize (as in the unstructured approach) then this combination approach may meet your need.

Start by completing the checklist and producing a MAP outline. Then working from the outline, add commentary and adjust the words in the outline to shape your approximated MAP to better fit you.

This will require effort but the process itself should result in additional understanding and insight.

Organic Approach (most detailed)

This last approach is how we, at People Management, write MAP reports. Working from the transcript, we write down all references to Circumstances, Abilities, Subject Matter, and Operating Relationship. We sift and sort and cluster. We always work from what the person has said.

We ask ourselves questions. For example, if someone says, "I influenced," we ask "How did he or she influence?" If the person says, "I planned," we look to see how he or she planned. We try to be as specific as the evidence allows us to be in describing how this individual went about accomplishing his or her achievements. Anything that doesn't recur at different points in a person's achievements is discarded. Categories, though, are expanded to capture the growth and development that takes place within people as they exercise their gifts.

Let me illustrate this point from the achievement examples of a person who derives satisfaction from the process of creating something.

> "Made unique designs using LEGO blocks . . . cut out shapes and put them on my ceiling that glowed in the dark . . . wrote poetry
> . . . watched how they danced and used what I saw to invent my
> own moves . . . made one of a kind pieces of pottery . . . mixed

ingredients in a new way . . . visualized an approach that had not been taken before . . . invented."

Can you see from these brief excerpts that this person enjoys designing, building, putting things together, shaping, and inventing, but the larger cluster and theme is one of creating?

In uncovering the Central Theme, we examine each achievement example and ask: What is this person doing? What is happening? What is this individual trying to accomplish? As a prospective theme appears, we test it by going back to each achievement and look for clear evidence to support it.

That is the process we use to come up with the MAP outline. We then write commentary that describes what those words represent. In writing this commentary, we try to connect and show the relationship between the various elements; i.e., this person is motivated to use these Abilities when dealing with this Subject Matter, under these Conditions when they can establish this Operating Relationship to others and accomplish the following Results.

Some Suggestions

Regardless of which method you choose to use, you may find it helpful to examine your data (tape, transcript, etc.) with the certain categorizations in mind. For example, in describing the Central Motivational Theme, ask yourself if the main theme involves:

- Looking good in comparison to others
- Exercising power and dominion over people, things, etc.
- Having an impact or effect on objects, people, organizations, etc.
- Accomplishing goals or targets
- Being engaged in a process of discovery, development or expression

When searching for the most descriptive motivated Abilities try describing how you are motivated to:
- Learn and understand
- Evaluate and decide

- Prepare, organize, and plan
- Take action
- Influence or inform others

Not everyone has motivated strengths in each category—stay with the facts. For example, some people speak very little about learning and focus mainly on implementation. Obviously learning takes place, but for purposes here, we would not describe the person as being motivated to learn.

In determining your motivated Subject Matter, it may be helpful to cluster your observations or thinking into the following:
- Intangibles, i.e., values, ideas, information, concepts
- Tangible things, i.e., vehicles, materials, sound, tools
- Data, i.e., numbers, words, logistics, facts
- People, i.e, individuals, cultures, groups
- Mechanisms, i.e, techniques, strategies, controls, models, technology, graphics

As you look to identify the Circumstances that are motivating to you, recognize that some conditions or factors trigger your motivation (get you started) and others tend to sustain it.

In broad terms, the types of Operating Relationships can be clustered into three categories:
- Contributor types
- Influencer types
- Overseer types

Relationship to Authority. In some Motivational Patterns, there appears to be a preferred relationship to authority that a person has—you may have a preference, also. You can think of this as a continuum ranging from complete independence throughout to continuous support. We have listed below some points on this continuum. If one fits you, then incorporate it into your understanding of your MAP.

Independent Throughout
Reacts to Initial Opportunity or Direction
Responds to Intermittent Support

Collaborative

Continuous Support

Resources. Two books have been written that provide more detail on how to develop Motivational Pattern information on your own. These are:

Who Do You Think You Are? by Dr. Nick Isbister and Dr. Martin Robinson. HarperCollins Publishers, 1999. Nick is the President of SIMA (UK) Ltd. in Oxford, UK, and the book was published in England.

The Truth About You by Arthur F. Miller Jr. and Ralph Mattson. Ten Speed Press, 1989. This book is out of print in the United States so it may be difficult to locate a copy. However, SIMA (Asia) Pte. Ltd. in Singapore has reprinted the book. John Samuels is President of the Singapore office.

Appendix B:

About People Management

People Management is an international consulting firm that specializes in job fit. We help individuals to make good decisions about their work and lives and help organizations make good decisions about people.

In 1961 Arthur F. Miller Jr., founder of People Management, developed the System for Identifying Motivated Abilities (SIMA) which identifies what a person is naturally motivated to do. Through SIMA, people discover their unique gifts which drive them to outstanding performance.

Organizations and individuals using SIMA have a competitive edge because they can assess "fit" and predict how optimal performance can be obtained.

At the time that this manuscript was prepared, People Management had offices and affiliations in Australia, Canada, England, Netherlands, New Zealand, Singapore, South Africa, Atlanta, Chicago, Dallas, Hartford, Lexington, Livermore, Madison, Minneapolis, Nashville, New York metro area, Philadelphia, Pittsburgh, Seattle, and St. Petersburg. Its corporate office is in Hartford (Avon), Connecticut.

Each office and affiliation is independently owned and focuses on applying SIMA to different applications. These include:

- Making better selection decisions (hiring, promotion, succession).
- Identifying the types of environments in which someone will best excel.
- Redesigning jobs to enhance job fit.

- Helping people to make better career and job fit decisions.
- Enhancing individual effectiveness.
- Enhancing team effectiveness.
- Helping to resolve conflict or performance problems.
- Identifying future leaders early in their careers.
- Improving one's ability to better manage himself or herself.
- Improving one's ability to better manage others.
- Developing critical job requirements and performance models.
- Assessing people against performance models and identifying areas of strength and potential weakness.
- Generating better candidates in executive search.
- Helping those in outplacement to better secure work that fits their Motivational Patterns.
- Helping those starting out in their work lives to make better career and educational decisions.
- Helping those who are in or approaching retirement to identify new vocational or avocational opportunities.

We believe that we can make a difference by understanding the complex dynamics of how people are motivated and gifted to achieve and help them and their organizations to shape the way they fit their jobs, environments and relationships.

Organizations that are licensed to use SIMA in their consulting activities:

Partner organizations:
  Innovative People Management, Ringwood, Australia
  PMI Shares, Inc., Avon, Connecticut
  People Management International Ltd., Wilmore, Kentucky
  People Management Mid-South, LLC, Nashville, Tennessee
  People Management Minnesota, Stillwater, Minnesota
  People Management Northeast, Avon, Connecticut
  SIMA (Asia) Pte. Ltd., Singapore
  SIMA (UK) Ltd., Oxford, UK

Affiliate, Associate, or other licensed organizations:
  Banis Consulting Group, Glenview, Illinois

Developing Learning Strategies, Nottingham, England
Emergo B.V., Bussum, Netherlands
The Hendricks Group, Dallas, Texas
Hunter People Management, Cardiff South, Australia
The InGenius Center Inc., Arlington Heights, Illinois
ITS Training, Essex, United Kingdom
J. Prinsloo Genote/Associates, Somerset West, South Africa
Lewis Training and Development, Middleton, Wisconsin
Marlys Hanson & Associates, Livermore, California
McMahon Associates, Vashon, Washington
Ministry By Design, Inc., Minneapolis, Minnesota
Obaniche Associates, Ottawa, Canada
Paris & Co., Monroe, Connecticut
Priority Consulting, Glen Ridge, New Jersey
Professional Resources Group, LLC, St. Petersburg, Florida
Richard M. Wellock Associates, Ligonier, Pennsylvania
SIMA New Zealand Ltd., Waikanae, New Zealand
The Strategic Source, Inc., West Point, Pennsylvania
Synergy Search, Inc., Alpharetta, Georgia

Contact information for any of the People Management locations can be obtained from:

People Management International, LLC
One Darling Drive
Avon Park South
Avon, CT 06001
(860) 678-8900
www.jobfit–pmi.com

Professionals interested in incorporating the SIMA process into their work or into their human resource functions should also contact the Director of Member Services at the above location.

Appendix C

Bibliography on SIMA

Bibliography: SIMA®

"Behavior Patterns Analyzed at Cargill," *The Career Development Bulletin*, Volume 3, Number 1, The Center for Research in Career Development, 1982.

Banis, William J. and Ronald L. Krannich, *Moving Out of Education*, Progressive Concepts, Inc., 1981, pp. 82-90.

Banis, William J., *A Preliminary Study of a Job: Analytic Inventory Derived From a Behavioral Consistency Method For Assessing Intrinsic Motivation*, doctoral dissertation, Old Dominion University, 1993.

Black, Thom with Lynda Stephenson, Born to Fly: *How to Discover and Encourage Your Child's Natural Gifts*, Zondervan Publishing House, Grand Rapids, Michigan, 1994.

Bondra, George, "Toward a Science of Persons: New Instrumentation for Understanding the Individual," Unpublished manuscript, 1984.

Bondra, George, "System for Identifying Motivated Abilities (SIMA®): Some Traditional Psychometric Issues," Unpublished manuscript, 1985.

Clarke, Susan, "Clear Skies for High Flyers," *Management Skills & Development*, April/May 1998, pp. 61-64.

Crites, John O., "A Validity and Reliability Study for Motivated Abilities Patterns," A research report submitted to a client, 1990.

Cunningham, James A., "The Perceived Effects of Applying a System for Identifying Motivated Abilities to the Problem of Job Misfit," doctoral dissertation, Institute of Advanced Studies, Walden University, 1985.

Darter, Steven M., "Bringing Career Development to Religious Communities," The Personnel and Guidance Journal, Volume 60, Number 5, January 1982.

Darter, Steven M., "Know Yourself Before You Go Job-Hunting," Imprint Newspapers, April 1985.

Darter, Steven M., "Save That Job: Transforming the Poor Performer," *Research Management,* Volume XXVIII, No. 3, May/June 1985.

Darter, Steven M., "How To Keep Careers On Track," *Motivation and Productivity,* PMI, Number 1, Fall 1990, p. 5.

Darter, Steven M., "Succession Planning Has Changed," *Motivation and Productivity*, Number 3, Spring 1992, p. 3.

Darter, Steven M., "People Perform Better When . . ." *Perspectives*, July 1997.

Dixon, Tony, "Working Happily," *Nursing Times,* July 3, 1985.

Dixon, Michael, "How People Show Their Real Working Strengths," *Financial Times*, London, No. 29,767, October 31, 1985.

Dixon, Michael, "Doing It For Kicks," *Business*, July 1991.

Forest, Robert B., "Go With the Flow," *Infosystems*, Perspective, September 1980.

Forest, Robert B., "Square Pegs in Round Holes?" *Infosystems*, Perspective, October 1980.

Hammond, Josh and James Morrison, *The Stuff Americans Are Made Of*, Macmillan, New York, 1996, pp. 48-55.

Hanson, Marlys, "Job Fit and Creativity," *IEEE Potentials Magazine*, October 1985.

Hanson, Marlys and Arthur F. Miller Jr., "Coaching for Career Development," Workshop Manual, 1992.

Hanson, Marlys and Arthur F. Miller Jr., "Job Fit and Career Management," Workshop Manual, 1992.

Hanson, Marlys and H. Fred Shultz, "Career Management System In Exxon Engineering: A Process for Learning and Leading," Eighth IEEE-USA Careers Conference, Ft. Worth, Texas, April 1994.

Hanson, Marlys and H. Fred Shultz, "Matching Employees to Their Work: A Mutually Beneficial Career Management System," Ninth IEEE-USA Careers Conference, Minneapolis, Minnesota, April 1996.

Isbister, Nick, "Beyond the Smile Factor," Motivation and Productivity, PMI, Number 3, Spring 1990, p. 7.

Isbister, Nick, "Is Society Slip Slidin' Away?" Irish National Conference of Institute for Personnel Management, published in *Business and Finance,* May 1990, pp. 3-7.

Isbister, Nick, "The Perils of Perestroika – Leading Culture-Change," *Motivation and Productivity,* PMI, Number 3, Spring, 1992, pp. 1-2.

Isbister, Nick, "Principles of Organisation Development and Their Relationship to SIMA," SIMA (UK) Ltd., Oxford, England, September 1999.

Isbister, Nick and Martin Robinson, *Who Do You Think You Are*, Harper Collins, London, England, 1999

Jorgensen, B.W., "SIMA® and Related Motivational Theory," Unpublished manuscript, 1979.

Kiel, Don, "How People Learn Influences Job Satisfaction and Job Productivity," *Motivation and Productivity*, PMI, Number 1, Fall 1990, p. 6.

Kuijk, Judith, "Wat is Jouw Motivatiepatroon?" *Observant*, March 21, 1996.

Marshall, Tom, *Understanding Leadership*, Lynnwood, WA, Emerald Books, Sovereign World Ltd., Chichester, England, 1991, pp. 183-188; 214-215.

Mattson, Ralph T. and Arthur F. Miller Jr., *Finding a Job You Can Love*, Thomas Nelson Publisher, Nashville, Tennessee, 1982.

Miller III, Arthur F., "Headhunting," *Nursing Times*, June 26, 1985.

Miller Jr., Arthur F., "Motivational Pattern Key to Productive Management of People," International Personnel Association, Yale Club, New York, 1971.

Miller Jr., Arthur F., "What Else," *The Colorado National Banks Quarterly*, Volume 3, June, 1978.

Miller Jr., Arthur F., "The Case for Management of Strengths," The National ASTD Convention, 1980.

Miller Jr., Arthur F., "The Dynamics of Motivational Patterns," *The Intercontinental Advanced Management Report*, Volume 2, No. 6, Krieger Publishing Company, 1980.

Miller Jr., Arthur F., "A Game Plan For the Interview," *Journal of College Placement*, Fall 1981.

Miller Jr., Arthur F., "Discover Your Design," CPC Annual, College Placement Council, Inc., 1984-85.

Miller Jr., Arthur F., "Look Down the Road," CPC Annual, College Placement Council, Inc., 1984-85.

Miller Jr., Arthur F., "Right for the Job?" *Nursing Times*, June 19, 1985.

Miller Jr., Arthur F., "Identifying Motivation To Minimize Mismatch," *Personnel Management*, October 1985.

Miller Jr., Arthur F., "When An Opening Occurs In the Executive Ranks," *International Business Communications, Ltd.,* London Press Center, London, 1986.

Miller Jr., Arthur F., "Build Your Search Around Your Giftedness," *Your Next Pastorate, Starting the Search,* The Alban Institute, Inc., Washington, D.C., 1990.

Miller Jr., Arthur F., "Rediscovering the Power of the Individual," National Conference, American Quality Foundation (ASQF), Atlanta, Georgia, April 1993.

Miller Jr., Arthur F., "Each Engineer A Unique Competitive Advantage," National Roundtable on Quality V; Rancho, Mirage, California, March 1994.

Miller Jr., Arthur F., "Designed to Shine: Patterns for Productivity," *Target,* Volume 12, Number 1, January/February/March 1996.

Miller Jr., Arthur F., "Surprised By Discovering Joy and Fulfilment in the Job," *ETHOS - Ethics in Business,* Oct/Nov 1997, pp. 8-10.

Miller Jr., Arthur F. and John O. Crites, SIMA *Theory and Research Handbook,* PMI Shares, Inc., 1991.

Miller Jr., Arthur F. and James A. Cunningham, "Avoiding Job Mismatches," *Management Digest,* American Management Associations, November 1981.

Miller Jr., Arthur F. and James A. Cunningham, "Managerial Misfits: Big Obstacle in Productivity Race," *AMA International Forum,* November 1981.

Miller Jr., Arthur F. and Marlys Hanson, "The Smile on the Face of a Leadership Tiger?" *Personnel Management,* October 1991, pp. 54-57.

Miller Jr., Arthur F. and Marlys Hanson, "Mismatches," *Across The Board,* June 2000, pp. 25-29.

Miller Jr., Arthur F. with William Hendricks, *Why You Can't Be Anything You Want To Be,* Zondervan Publishing House, Grand Rapids, Michigan, 1999.

Miller Jr., Arthur F. and Ralph T. Mattson, *The Truth About You*, Ten Speed Press, Berkeley, California, 1989.

Moneymaker, Jonathan, "Unique Perspectives on Communication," *Motivation and Productivity,* PMI, Number 4, 1992, pp. 4-5.

Monnik, R., "De Succesfactor in Elke Loopbaan: Motivatie," *Loopbaangids NOBOL,* 1997.

Moorby, Ed, *How to Succeed in Employee Development: Moving From Vision to Results,* McGraw-Hill, Berkshire, United Kingdom, 1991, p. 6, 65.

Philips, Anton F., "Het Motivatiepatroon," *ELAN*, interview by Ronald Buitendam, April 1995.

Philips, Anton F., "Motivatie Analyse als Onderdeel van MD-Beleid," *MD Journal,* September 1995.

Philips, Anton F. and Frits Philips Jr., "De Philips Traditie," *FEM*, interview by Sander Wieringa, January 6, 1996.

Rogers, J. L., "An Analysis of Motivational Patterns of Managers and Technical Professionals in a Manufacturing and Development Installation," master's dissertation, Massachusetts Institute of Technology, 1986.

Sherman, Doug and William Hendricks, *Your Work Matters to God*, Navpress, Colorado Springs, Colorado, 1987, pp. 138-139.

Smith, Marvin A., "Selection and Orientation of Missionaries For the Navigators," master's thesis, Fuller Theological Seminary, June 1983.

Staub, Dick and Jeff Trautman, *Intercristo's Career Kit: A Christian's Guide to Career Building*, Intercristo, Seattle, Washington, 1985.

Stork, Peter, "Culture-Change," *Motivation and Productivity*, PMI, Number 3, Spring 1992.

Stork, Peter, "Unleashing People's Talent," *Management*, July 1997, pp. 27-28.

Taylor, Michael D., "To Find the Best Sales Managers, Look Beyond Job Performance," *The Culpepper Letter*, July 1990.

Taylor, Michael D., "How ASYNC Dealt with A Sales Rep Hiring Dilemma," *The Culpepper Letter*, November 1990.

Uijl, Stella E. den, "De SIMA-Methode: een Systeem voor het Identificeren van Motivatiepatronen," *Kluwer: Methoden, Technieken en Analyses*, Volume 33, 1995.

Uijl, Stella E. den and Anton F. Philips, "Identificeren van Motivatiepatronen," *Gids voor Personeelsmanagement*, February 1995.

Uijl, Stella E. den and Anton F. Philips, "Natuurlijk Talent Optimaal Inzetten," *Dagelijks Beleid*, December 1996.

Welch, Barry, *Managing To Make Organisations Work*, Hempstead, Hertfordshire, England: Director Books, Fitzwilliam Publishing Limited, 1992, pp. 94-99.

Wolf, Dr. Billy, "A Dream Job, It's Within You," *The New Paper*, Singapore, December 1985.

Appendix D:

Summary of Research on SIMA and Motivational Patterning

Summary of Research

1961 – 1981

- During the initial twenty years of SIMA®'s development, efforts to validate the accuracy, usefulness and predictive nature of SIMA consisted of participant scoring on one or another variation of evaluative instruments which essentially asked participants if they and others agreed with the findings and if the participant would use the information to make key decisions. In addition, supervisors of the individual were also asked through a similar questionnaire to affirm or question the accuracy of the data. During this time period, thousands of people were surveyed and not one person wrote that SIMA had not captured the essential accuracy of that person's strengths. The results are a form of content validity and convergent (concurrent) validity.

- From 1976-1981 SIMA was used by Lawrence Livermore National Laboratory as the primary method of assessment in its career/life planning workshop. The effectiveness of the workshop was evaluated through a questionnaire sent to each participant and his or her supervisor one year after participation. In total, 750 employees were involved. The questionnaires produced the following results.

  – 86% of the participants reported that their morale had improved.
  – 66% of the supervisors reported improved morale.

- 68% of the participants reported improved communication with supervisors.
- 54% of the supervisors reported improved communication.

In the first survey (1976), 53% of the supervisors felt that the Laboratory would recover the cost of sending the employee to the workshop, and by 1980, that number had steadily increased to 88%.

1981 - 1986

- Testing the predictive validity of SIMA, a doctoral dissertation (Cunningham, 1985) provided statistically significant results of the perceived relationship between SIMA and the critical requirements of the job. The subjects were 81 individuals who had participated in the SIMA process as part of an outplacement process. An anonymous questionnaire was used as the measure. There was a positive Pearson product-moment correlation (r -.50; p .001) between Job Performance (i.e., job satisfaction, job productivity, promotion/recognition, and salary increments) and the perceived use of the SIMA process. With respect to the dimension of Job Relations, defined as relationships with superiors, peers, and subordinates, a positive Pearson product-moment correlation (r = .41; p .001) was also found that was statistically significant.

- A program to develop reliable guidelines for the hiring or promotion into the position of head nurse for a large Midwestern teaching hospital (Wesley Medical Center) used SIMA to evaluate 40 former or present head nurses. The task was to identify those effective or clearly ineffective at the job of head nursing. Management rated the 40 participants and slotted each person into an overall category of effective or clearly ineffective. SIMA identified 80% of those determined by management as effective or as clearly ineffective.

- A concurrent validity study to build guidelines for the selection of missionaries (The Navigators) followed a similar methodology. Management defined critical criteria and rated each former or current missionary in the study as being successful or ineffective. Use of SIMA on couples achieved an accuracy rate of 81% in both groupings (n = 21 couples) but was 91% when evaluating the men who were or were not successful (n = 237).

• A study of 265 employees of a large computer manufacturer (IBM) undertaken as part of a master's thesis (Rogers, 1986) stated that surveys of participants regarding the accuracy of SIMA and MAPs achieved over a 98% positive rating on all dimensions.

• A test of SIMA to determine its ability to identify highly successful large city sales managers for a major life insurance company (New York Life Insurance Company) achieved impressive results as long as the issue was highly successful or unsuccessful. Attempts to place each of 24 managers into performance quintiles using SIMA based on a variety of quantified performance measurements, were less successful; 18 out of 24 were in the quintile. A revision of the evaluation criteria using SIMA was able to accurately "classify" all but one of the 24.

1989 - 1999

• In the spring of 1989, an extensive research program—The Leadership Profile Project —was launched by "a large Midwestern Fortune 100 company associated with manufacturing and technology," (McDonnell Douglas) to evaluate empirically the usefulness of SIMA for identifying potential leaders for executive and managerial positions. The research design followed the test standards established by the American Psychological Association (1985) for determining the psychometric characteristics of assessment techniques (i.e., scoring, objectivity, reliability, and validity). There were seven studies conducted to appraise the extent to which SIMA approximated the APA Standards. The principal investigator was the nationally known testing psychologist, Dr. John Crites. Dr. Crites is the author of a number of standard textbooks on both psychometric testing and assessment methodology.

Specifically, the company wanted the following questions answered:

- Can the MAP® profile be used as a reliable selection tool?

- Can the MAP be used to identify leaders who best demonstrate TQMS behaviors?

- Are individual MAPs stable over time?

Dr. Crites concluded that the results of the studies provided the answers to these questions. He felt that SIMA was both theoretically sound and empirically reliable and valid for use as a selection tool; met the applicable standards, as enumerated by the American Psychological Association, for the assessment and selection of leaders and that the individual MAP profiles are stable over time.

The results of Dr. Crites's studies are:

- SIMA had an "exceptionally high" interscorer agreement of 90 percent. This means that SIMA analysts, working independently, scored the profile items in the same way 90 percent of the time. Dr. Crites considered this "level of objectivity as outstanding."

- SIMA reliability (i.e., it gives the same results over time) was "quite high." SIMA showed "marked stability" when participants were "re-Mapped" after a five-year interim period.

- SIMA was seen as suitable "for measuring TQMS behaviors." This was supported by "substantial content validity," and the "exceptionally high" 81 percent agreement attained by three independent judges in their ratings of the relationship of SIMA leadership behaviors to TQMS leadership behaviors.

- SIMA achieved generally positive results in one sample of the criterion-related validity study, but not in the second sample. Dr. Crites felt that this was possibly due to supervisor difference in their ratings using a fairly complex experimental listing of SIMA-type work behaviors. In the first sample, "substantial agreement" existed between the scores given on the MAP report and subsequent performance ratings given by a supervisor.

- SIMA demonstrated reliability and validity "equal to, if not greater than, that of assessment centers"—based on critical literature reviews of the latter.

- SIMA "conformed closely" to the motivational model upon which it is based, and to the Leadership Profile used by the company.

- Participants in SIMA gave a "highly favorable" evaluation of the usefulness of SIMA for themselves and for their company.

- In summary, Dr. Crites wrote that SIMA achieved "positive results" in all studies He saw this as a "unique and highly positive outcome for this type of project." He further wrote that "The weight of the evidence for these findings is indeed impressive," concluding that "SIMA can be used with confidence as a selection and leadership identification method."

John O. Crites earned his Ph.D. in Counseling Psychology from Columbia University and has held full professorships and visiting scholar positions at various institutions including: Northwestern, Iowa, Berkeley, Maryland, and Kent State. He has numerous honors including: APGA Research Award, ASTD's Walter Storey Award, and NVGA's Eminent Career Award. At the time that this document was prepared, he had authored 4 books, 15 book chapters, 7 monographs, 34 articles, 26 books and test reviews and has made 49 presentations. He has also developed 7 tests, and at the time this document was prepared, he was under contract with Prentice Hall to write a book entitled: *Test Psychology: The Measurement of Abilities, Interests and Personality.*

- In 1993, a Ph.D. dissertation was completed by William J. Banis at Old Dominion University, which sought to determine if SIMA, when used as a job analysis tool, had acceptable internal reliability and an ability to differentiate among occupational groups. The

SIMA taxonomy of 268 behavioral elements was reconstituted in a Job Specifications Inventory (JSI) and administered to 614 subject matter experts in seven occupational groups—certified public accountants, civil engineers, elementary teachers, insurance sales agents, musicians, personnel managers, and secretaries.

Banis found that the JSI had demonstrated high internal validity with reliability estimates in the mid to high .90 range and that the JSI was able to find similarities and differences among occupations. Banis concluded that the JSI had utility as a job analysis tool and, in particular, had utility in selection, placement and career management applications.

• Exxon Research and Engineering has offered a career management workshop since 1989 to supervisors and employees where SIMA® was the key assessment tool used. During 1994, research was presented at an IEEE Conference covering the years 1992-1994 evaluating the success of the workshop. Reported results were:

  – 66% - 72% of employees were satisfied with the process.
  – 60% - 86% of employees were satisfied with their career plan.
  – 68% - 77% of employees were satisfied with supervisor interaction in developing their career plan.
  – 67% - 79% of managers felt employees had more effective career goals.
  – 69% - 76% of managers felt they had more effective career discussions with their employees.
  – 74% - 87% of managers felt the workshop helped them as supervisors in doing career discussions.
  – 70% - 79% of the managers were satisfied with the process.

• During 1999, People Management Northeast completed 132 formal MAP profiles and all participants were surveyed as to the accuracy and value of their MAPs.

  – 100% of the participants "strongly agreed" or "agreed" that their reports were an accurate description of what motivated them to perform at their best.

– On each dimension of value (i.e., as a resource when evaluating the job fit aspects of a promotion or when asked to come up with a self-development plan or as a tool to help an employee and his or her manager to understand each other or in helping to resolve conflicts or misunderstandings or to help a team to function more effectively), 86% - 95% of the participants either "strongly agreed" or "agreed" that SIMA would be beneficial (depending upon the question).

Acknowledgements of Appreciation

There are many people I would like to publicly acknowledge. As I look through the words and presentation of this book, I can easily see places where all I did was borrow or modify what others within People Management have said, written, or done. In addition to Art Miller Jr., whose work I have heavily relied upon, his son and my business partner, Kim Miller, has so often been the brains behind new insights. Kim shies away from recognition, so he is frequently not given the credit he deserves. Within this book, I see the hands of Peter Stork (retired head of People Management's operation in Australia); Dr. Nick Isbister (SIMA UK - England); Rob Stevenson (People Management Minnesota); Rick Wellock (Ligonier, Pennsylvania); Jonathan Moneymaker, who built a series of workbooks for PMI; Shawn Carroll and people at the Disney Institute who designed a program using SIMA® called "The Stuff Americans are Made Of[SM]"; Ralph Mattson, whose creativity was employed at People Management for many years; Arthur Miller III (PMI, Ltd. - Kentucky); my daughter, Katie, who on occasion joined me in the wee hours of the morning and provided some fresh insight; my son, Kevin, who continually challenged me to think about my beliefs; and my parents, who taught me to love life and love myself. I would also like to thank two writers who were instrumental in shaping an earlier version of this book: Bill Peel of The Paul Taurnier Institute and Andrew Julian of The Hartford Courant. Let me finish by acknowledging my assistant, Diane Cables, who puts up with my somewhat chaotic ways and continual edits; my wife, Diane, who is my life partner, soul mate, and balance; and to all the clients with whom I have worked and counseled, who opened their hearts and minds and have shared with me their work and life experiences and have provided an education that I could never have dreamed of obtaining.

The Agreement Between You and People Management

In this book, I have presented a significant amount of proprietary, trade secret and copyrighted material and concepts. I have done this because I want you to benefit in your life as many thousands already have.

Although I encourage you to use the concept and processes expressed in this book, you need to remember that you cannot reproduce, copy or otherwise duplicate, or distribute, lend or transfer any part of the contents of this book without the express written permission of People Management.

I welcome you to benefit from the contents and concepts personally and to express and share those benefits in all aspects of your life, but People Management is not giving you permission to resell, modify and sell, or repackage and sell the materials. Therefore, you cannot deliver the materials themselves, either reproduced or modified, as part of any seminar, training program, workshop, consulting or similar business activity which you may make available to your employer, clients or to the public for the purpose of financial gain. You also need to understand that should you wish to use any materials either directly or indirectly in such a seminar, training program, workshop, consulting or similar business activity that you might make available to your employer, clients, or to the public for the purpose of financial gain at any time, you must first obtain written consent from People Management.

"SIMA" (the System for Identifying Motivated Abilities) and "MAP" (Motivated Abilities Pattern) are registered Trademarks, and "Achievement Interviewing" is a registered Service Mark of PMI Shares, Inc.

About the Author

Steven M. Darter is President of People Management Northeast. Prior to joining People Management, Steve was on the staff and faculty at Saint Joseph College (CT) where he was the Director of the Career Planning and Placement Office and taught the career counseling sequence in the graduate counseling program. He also worked in insurance sales and held management positions in retailing before attending graduate school.

Steve started his consulting career with People Management in 1976. In 1984 he was appointed Senior Vice President and head of executive search and selection, in 1990 President of PMI Northeast, and from 1996-1999, served as the first Chairman of People Management International, L.L.C. (PMI's partnership organization). He has an M.S. in Education and an Ed.S. in Counseling and Personnel from the State University of New York (SUNY) at Albany. His B.S. is in Sociology from SUNY at Oswego.

Steve has been a guest speaker/facilitator at seminars, appeared on radio talk shows, authored several articles, served as Vice Chairman of the Greater Hartford Chamber of Commerce's Technology Council and has been profiled as one of North America's top executive recruiters in the book, *The New Career Makers*, based upon survey results of CEOs, senior HR executives, and other business leaders.

Steve specializes in executive search, selection, succession, executive development, and consultation on issues related to "job fit" and the effective utilization of employee strengths.

People Management was founded in 1961 and has offices and affiliations in twenty-eight locations throughout the world. For close to forty years, PMI has focused its business applications on "job fit" – helping organizations to improve results through a better understanding and positioning of people and helping people to make good decisions about work.

Spread the Word

To arrange for a presentation or seminar on SIMA and *Managing Yourself, Managing Others,* contact: Steve Darter at (860) 678-8900, extension 3007.

To order additional copies of *Managing Yourself, Managing Others* at a quantity discount, contact either Steve Darter or Diane Cables at People Management (860) 678-8900 or the publisher, Brian Jud, at Publishing Directions (860-276-2452).